CONTEMPORARY
ISSUES
COMPANION

Steroids

Other Books of Related Interest:

Opposing Viewpoints Series

Medicine

Teen Drug Abuse

At Issue Series

Child Athletes

Extreme Sports

Performance Enhancing Drugs

Should College Athletes Be Paid?

Steroids

Stefan Kiesbye, Book Editor

GREENHAVEN PRESS
A part of Gale, Cengage Learning

Detroit • New York • San Francisco • New Haven, Conn • Waterville, Maine • London

GALE
CENGAGE Learning™

Christine Nasso, *Publisher*
Elizabeth Des Chenes, *Managing Editor*

© 2007 Greenhaven Press, a part of Gale, Cengage Learning.

For more information, contact:
Greenhaven Press
27500 Drake Rd.
Farmington Hills, MI 48331-3535
Or you can visit our Internet site at gale.cengage.com

Articles in Greenhaven Press anthologies are often edited for length to meet page require-
ments. In addition, original titles of these works are changed to clearly present the main
thesis and to explicitly indicate the author's opinion. Every effort is made to ensure that
Greenhaven Press accurately reflects the original intent of the authors. Every effort has
been made to trace the owners of copyrighted material.

Cover photograph reproduced by permission of Gstar.

LIBRARY OF CONGRESS CATALOGING-IN-PUBLICATION DATA

Steroids / Stefan Kiesbye, book editor.
p. cm. -- (Contemporary issues companion)
Includes bibliographical references and index.
ISBN-13: 978-0-7377-3709-7 (hardcover)
ISBN-10: 0-7377-3709-3 (hardcover)
ISBN-13: 978-0-7377-3710-3 (pbk.)
ISBN-10: 0-7377-3710-7 (pbk.)
1. Anabolic steroids. 2. Doping in sports. I. Kiesbye, Stefan.
RC1230.S732 2008
362.29--dc22

2007023062

Printed in the United States of America
2 3 4 5 6   12 11 10 09 08

ED081

Contents

Chapter 3: Perspectives On Steroid Use

Chapter 4: How Should Society Deal with Steroid Use?

Foreword

In the news, on the streets, and in neighborhoods, individuals are confronted with a variety of social problems. Such problems may affect people directly: A young woman may struggle with depression, suspect a friend of having bulimia, or watch a loved one battle cancer. And even the issues that do not directly affect her private life—such as religious cults, domestic violence, or legalized gambling—still impact the larger society in which she lives. Discovering and analyzing the complexities of issues that encompass communal and societal realms as well as the world of personal experience is a valuable educational goal in the modern world.

Effectively addressing social problems requires familiarity with a constantly changing stream of data. Becoming well informed about today's controversies is an intricate process that often involves reading myriad primary and secondary sources, analyzing political debates, weighing various experts' opinions—even listening to firsthand accounts of those directly affected by the issue. For students and general observers, this can be a daunting task because of the sheer volume of information available in books, periodicals, on the evening news, and on the Internet. Researching the consequences of legalized gambling, for example, might entail sifting through congressional testimony on gambling's societal effects, examining private studies on Indian gaming, perusing numerous Web sites devoted to Internet betting, and reading essays written by lottery winners as well as interviews with recovering compulsive gamblers. Obtaining valuable information can be time-consuming—since it often requires researchers to pore over numerous documents and commentaries before discovering a source relevant to their particular investigation.

Greenhaven's Contemporary Issues Companion series seeks to assist this process of research by providing readers with useful and pertinent information about today's complex issues. Each volume in this anthology series focuses on a topic of current interest, presenting informative and thought-provoking selections written from a wide variety of viewpoints. The readings selected by the editors include such diverse sources as personal accounts and case studies, pertinent factual and statistical articles, and relevant commentaries and overviews. This diversity of sources and views, found in every Contemporary Issues Companion, offers readers a broad perspective in one convenient volume.

In addition, each title in the Contemporary Issues Companion series is designed especially for young adults. The selections included in every volume are chosen for their accessibility and are expertly edited in consideration of both the reading and comprehension levels of the audience. The structure of the anthologies also enhances accessibility. An introductory essay places each issue in context and provides helpful facts such as historical background or current statistics and legislation that pertain to the topic. The chapters that follow organize the material and focus on specific aspects of the book's topic. Every essay is introduced by a brief summary of its main points and biographical information about the author. These summaries aid in comprehension and can also serve to direct readers to material of immediate interest and need. Finally, a comprehensive index allows readers to efficiently scan and locate content.

The Contemporary Issues Companion series is an ideal launching point for research on a particular topic. Each anthology in the series is composed of readings taken from an extensive gamut of resources, including periodicals, newspapers, books, government documents, the publications of private and public organizations, and Internet Web sites. In these volumes, readers will find factual support suitable for use in reports, debates, speeches, and research papers. The anthologies also facilitate further research, featuring a book and periodical bibliography and a list of organizations to contact for additional information.

A perfect resource for both students and the general reader, Greenhaven's Contemporary Issues Companion series is sure to be a valued source of current, readable information on social problems that interest young adults. It is the editors' hope that readers will find the Contemporary Issues Companion series useful as a starting point to formulate their own opinions about and answers to the complex issues of the present day.

Introduction

In 1994 Major League Baseball (MLB) was at the brink of irrelevance. That year's strike accomplished what even World War II had failed to do: It canceled, for the first time in history, the World Series. Fans' bitterness led to apathy and cynicism. Both owners and players were accused of greed, and when the sport finally returned late the next year, not many truly cared.

Then in 1998 Mark McGwire and Sammy Sosa brought baseball back. The two sluggers took a run at one of baseball's most hallowed records and threatened to surpass Roger Maris' single season homerun record of sixty-one. The nation was spellbound. Owners' profits and players' salaries were forgiven, as these two men swatted home run after home run. The record chase inspired fans and fueled water-cooler discussions. In the end, both players broke the old record, and Mark McGwire set a new one with seventy homers (bested in 2001 by Barry Bonds's seventy-three).

Steroids in Baseball

Soon after, the explosion of the long ball and the bulky physiques of players who had started their careers noticeably smaller in stature led to a major controversy that has since devastated baseball and taken its toll in many other sports. Steroids, it was claimed, were behind the fabulous new records. What had long been known in locker rooms now made its way into newspapers' headlines: Steroids could help athletes train harder and longer, help them gain weight, bulk up, and achieve super stardom. If aspiring athletes wanted to sign a big contract, they had to be big.

"Big Mac" McGwire suddenly did not look so invincible anymore, and the public started to look with suspicion at the muscular arms and outsized chests of their favorite hitters.

Even in 1998, McGwire's achievements had been questioned, and he admitted to the use of Androstenedione, a legal dietary supplement that had been banned by both the National Football League (NFL) and the International Olympic Committee (IOC). Only the euphoria of the record chase had silenced doubters that year.

As the debate over the fairness and legality of steroids and Andro grew (both had never been banned by MLB), it also became apparent to the public that steroids had long been part of professional sports. Bodybuilders knew the positive effects on mind and body and had used them ever since the glory days from 1970 to 1980 when Arnold Schwarzenegger won the Mr. Olympia title seven times. The Austrian bodybuilder admitted freely to steroid use and publicly stated that he thought it made sense to use something that would give a person an advantage over his rivals.

In baseball, amphetamines (stimulants, sometimes called "greenies") had once been the drug of choice; now it was steroids. Yet the angry and disappointed fans were suddenly turned off by sky-rocketing homerun counts—everyone who hit a large number of long balls was subject to suspicion.

Younger Athletes Using

What was more alarming than steroid use by professional athletes was the discovery that college players and high school athletes also took performance-enhancing drugs to gain muscle mass and scholarships. Cheating professionals were one thing, but teenage delinquents another. If unpaid amateurs, the backbone of athletics, already took drugs, then all sports, it seemed, had been corrupted. In addition to ethical questions concerning steroid use, the health of young users became a subject of debate. Drug-related deaths of student athletes at all levels highlighted just how serious the problem was.

Many blamed major league players for this development, saying the players were bad role models for teenagers who were trying to emulate them. Others accused the general public of relishing home runs and super feats, which could only be performed if the athlete took steroids. Steroids have been in the general population for roughly three decades, and from the hulking East German swimmers of the 1980s to the eye-popping feats of Yankees player Jason Giambi or bodybuilder Arnold Schwarzenegger, they have influenced the perception of human limits.

The congressional hearing of March 17, 2005, during which several baseball players and executives testified, shed little light on the subject. Jose Canseco, the colorful and outspoken ex-player accused many of his former teammates of "juicing" the game, yet most of the subpoenaed players and executives denied the use of steroids and/or denied knowledge of steroid use. Congress struggled to assert some authority over the situation, but in the end gained little control.

Taking Another Look at Steroid Use

It might take an unbiased look at steroids to find a solution that is not merely punitive. Athletes in the early 2000s take many dietary supplements to enhance their physical development, and it may be useful to ask where exactly the line distinguishing positive from negative should be drawn amid the wide variety of drugs. Are steroids really as dangerous to athletes as has been claimed, or is it the abuse of players without any medical knowledge that has led to the drug-related deaths of several? Perhaps a more important question concerns why people place such importance on sports in general and on winning in particular.

If the public can take a step back from condemning individual athletes for taking banned drugs, it might discover the larger picture and find out why athletes feel the need to sidestep the rules. People might come to a better understanding of how the long and cheerful summer nights of 1998 and fans' enthusiasm for Sosa and McGwire are connected to the deaths of relatively obscure pitchers or unknown college players. Steroids are only the latest incarnation of substances athletes use to gain a competitive advantage. Maybe people have to rethink their position on records and have to investigate their own parts in that larger picture, if they want to keep steroids out of children's locker rooms and in the hands of medical professionals who administer them in only certain prescribed cases.

CHAPTER 1

What Are Steroids and Why Are They Used?

History and Use of Steroids

Office of National Drug Control Policy

This selection provides an overview of anabolic steroids, their history, use, production, and their considerable health risks. Not only are steroids widely available in sports, but the White House Office of National Drug Control Policy (ONDCP) finds that their use is widespread among teenagers and young adults. Steroids, which can be injected, applied to the skin, or taken orally, have found their way into school gyms and college locker rooms.

The ONDCP is a component of the Executive Office of the President, and was established by the Anti-Drug Abuse Act of 1988. The principal purpose of ONDCP is to establish policies, priorities, and objectives for the nation's drug control program. The goals of the program are to reduce illicit drug use, manufacturing, and trafficking, drug-related crime and violence, and drug-related health consequences.

Overview

Anabolic steroids were developed in the late 1930s primarily to treat hypogonadism, a condition in which the testes do not produce sufficient testosterone for normal growth, development, and sexual functioning. The primary medical uses of these compounds are to treat delayed puberty, some types of impotence, and wasting of the body caused by HIV infection or other diseases.

During the 1930s, scientists discovered that anabolic steroids could facilitate the growth of skeletal muscle in laboratory animals. This led to abuse of these compounds by bodybuilders and weightlifters and then by athletes in other sports.

Anabolic steroids can be taken orally, injected intramuscularly, or rubbed on the skin when in the form of gels or

Office of National Drug Control Policy, "Steroids Overview," www.whitehousedrug policy.gov, December 31, 2006.

15

creams. These drugs are often used in patterns called cycling, which involves taking multiple doses of steroids over a specific period of time, stopping for a period, and starting again. Users also frequently combine several different types of steroids in a process known as stacking. By doing this, users believe that the different steroids will interact to produce an effect on muscle size that is greater than the effects of using each drug individually.

Another mode of steroid use is "pyramiding." This is a process in which users slowly escalate steroid use (increasing the number of drugs used at one time and/or the dose and frequency of one or more steroids) reaching a peak amount at mid-cycle and gradually tapering the dose toward the end of the cycle.

Extent of Use

Results from the 2006 Monitoring the Future Study, which surveys students in eighth, tenth, and twelfth grades, show that 1.6% of eighth graders, 1.8% of tenth graders, and 2.7% of twelfth graders reported using steroids at least once in their lifetimes.

Regarding the ease by which one can obtain steroids, 17.1% of eighth graders, 30.2% of tenth graders, and 41.1% of twelfth graders surveyed in 2006 reported that steroids were "fairly easy" or "very easy" to obtain. Furthermore, 60.2% of twelfth graders surveyed reported that using steroids was a "great risk" during 2006.

The Centers for Disease Control and Prevention (CDC) also conducts a survey of high school students throughout the United States, the Youth Risk Behavior Surveillance System (YRBSS). Nearly 5% of all high school students surveyed by CDC in 2005 reported lifetime use of steroid pills/shots without a doctor's prescription.

Approximately 1.9% of young adults (ages 19–28) surveyed in 2005 reported lifetime use of steroids.

Health Effects

Anabolic steroid abuse has been associated with a wide range of adverse side effects ranging from some that are physically unattractive, such as acne and breast development in men, to others that are life threatening. Most of the effects are reversible if the abuser stops taking the drug, but some can be permanent. In addition to the physical effects, anabolic steroids can also cause increased irritability and aggression.

Some of the health consequences that can occur in both males and females include liver cancer, heart attacks, and elevated cholesterol levels. In addition to this, steroid use among adolescents may prematurely stop the lengthening of bones resulting in stunted growth.

People who inject steroids also run the risk of contracting or transmitting hepatitis or HIV. Some steroid abusers experience withdrawal symptoms when they stop taking the drug. These withdrawal symptoms include mood swings, fatigue, restlessness, loss of appetite, insomnia, reduced sex drive, and depression. This depression can lead to suicide attempts, and if left untreated, can persist for a year or more after the abuser stops taking the drugs.

Production & Trafficking

Illicit anabolic steroids are often sold at gyms, competitions, and through mail operations after being smuggled into this country. The most common sources for obtaining steroids for illegal use are Internet purchases and smuggling them into the U.S. from other countries such as Mexico and European countries. These countries do not require a prescription for the purchase of steroids, making it easier to smuggle them. In addition to this, steroids are also illegally diverted from U.S. pharmacies or synthesized in clandestine [secret] laboratories.

Legislation

Concerns over a growing illicit market and prevalence of abuse combined with the possibility of harmful long-term effects of steroid use led Congress to place anabolic steroids into Schedule III of the Controlled Substances Act (CSA) in 1991. It is therefore illegal to possess or sell anabolic steroids without a valid prescription. Some States have also implemented additional fines and penalties for illegal use of anabolic steroids.

The International Olympic Committee, National Collegiate Athletic Association and many professional sports leagues (including the Major League Baseball, National Basketball Association, National Football League, and National Hockey League), have banned the use of steroids by athletes due to their potentially dangerous side effects and because they give the user an unfair advantage.

Street Terms for Steroids

- Arnolds

- Gym Candy

- Juice

- Pumpers

- Stackers

- Weight Trainers

The Goals and Risks of Bulking Up

Cynthia Kuhn, Scot Swartzwelder, and Wilkie Wilson

The authors of this selection list the different steroids available as of 2000, discuss the benefits and risks for men, women, and adolescents, and shed light on possible psychological effects and addiction. Cynthia Kuhn and Wilkie Wilson are professors of pharmacology at Duke University Medical Center. Scott Swartzwelder is a professor of psychology at the same institution.

Athletes want drugs that they can take during training to increase muscle mass and strength, and they prefer drugs that are either legal or undetectable at the time of performance (or testing). The drugs listed in this chapter are all used for this purpose. Some of them do work, but any drug that is effective is (1) probably dangerous to the user and (2) illegal in most competitive environments. Anabolic drugs increase production of protein in the muscle. Some act as natural hormones to stimulate protein synthesis (the making of proteins). These include anabolic steroids, growth hormone, and insulin. Others like clenbuterol and GHB [gama hydroxybutyric acid, a synthetic depressant], allegedly stimulate the body to produce more of these hormones on its own. Finally, nutritional supplements that are supposed to provide more amino acids, the building blocks of protein, are widely touted as safe, natural ways to augment muscle growth. Recently, a flood of trace nutrients have joined the amino acids as nutritional supplements to increase muscle mass.

Anabolic Steroids

Anabolic steroids were probably the first drugs that athletes of the modern era used to enhance athletic performance. *Anabolic steroids* are natural hormones produced by the body that help build muscle. The male sex hormone testosterone is the most active anabolic steroid in the human body. Cortisol, the stress hormone produced by the adrenal gland, is also a steroid, but it is a *catabolic steroid* that tears muscle down. Steroid hormones used to treat asthma are variations of cortisol, and these have no anabolic effects, so you don't have to worry that you are taking banned steroids if you are just treating your asthma. In fact, the high doses of these catabolic steroids that are used to treat autoimmune diseases produce muscle loss as a severe side effect.

Men have bigger muscles than women because their bodies produce much more of the male hormone testosterone. When boys go through puberty, their testicles produce more testosterone, which triggers the rapid increase in height and muscle mass that boys experience. Testosterone treatment can help boys with underdeveloped testicles go through normal puberty. The idea that testosterone could increase muscle mass in athletes was a natural extension of our knowledge of how normal male bodies develop.

Anabolic steroids affect more than muscle mass. The term *anabolic* is really a bit of a misnomer [misleading name] because testosterone mainly facilitates reproduction. Testosterone is an important part of sperm production and helps to create secondary sexual characteristics in men, including male-pattern facial, chest, and limb hair, male-pattern baldness, male-type body odor, and increased sweating. You may remember the adage of a bygone era that men sweat but women perspire. Testosterone, not ladylike behavior, is what's responsible for the larger number of sweat glands and greater volume of sweat that men produce. Testosterone increases the size of the larynx, leading to the deeper voice of adult men, and creates more red blood cells. Testosterone also changes the pattern of blood lipids to one that is more likely to lead to the development of cardiovascular disease. Given all of these natural effects of testosterone, it's not surprising that there is no such thing as a purely "anabolic" steroid that can stimulate muscle growth without causing all the other effects of testosterone. These other effects contribute to many of the dangerous consequences of anabolic steroid use in sports.

The "good" effects of anabolic steroids cannot be separated from the "bad" effects of testosterone because testosterone receptors that build muscles are exactly like the receptors that enlarge the larynx or cause hair loss. Therefore, any drug that works in the muscle also works elsewhere in the body.

Normal Effects of Testosterone-Like Hormones

Puberty: sexual development, increase in height, muscle deposition, hair development, deepening of voice

Reproduction: libido, sperm production

Circulation: red blood cell formation, clotting factors, blood volume

The Use of Anabolic Steroids in Sports

Russian weight lifters in the 1954 world weight lifting competition introduced anabolic steroids to international athletic competition. This practice was widely adopted, including by American coaches, and by the 1964 Olympics, the practice was widespread. The East German women's swim teams of the 1960s through the 1980s dominated the sport—and for good reason. They received injections of testosterone throughout their training. Women's bodies normally produce only a tiny amount of testosterone. The huge increase in testosterone these women received let them develop muscles much bigger than women typically can, even during intensive weight training. Upper-body muscle mass generally translates into improved swimming times, and these women showed dramatically improved performance. The Chinese women's swim team in the Los Angeles Olympics tried the same strategy. Again, their upper body mass increased, and swimming times decreased. Unfortunately, they misjudged the greatly improved sensitivity of the testing technique. Steroids were detected in a number of these athletes, and they were disqualified.

The benefit of anabolic steroids to women athletes is clear because even small amounts of testosterone are way above the typical levels for women. But what about normal men who have already gone through puberty? Science took us a step backward here. For years, scientists stated that carefully conducted laboratory research could not show that anabolic steroids cause any improvement of performance in normal men. At the same time, weight lifters and other athletes were touting their benefits. Both the scientists and weight lifters were right. Under normal circumstances, men produce so much testosterone that even doubling or tripling testosterone levels really doesn't help. This is exactly what the "careful scientific studies" did. Furthermore, they put the subjects on an exercise regimen at the same time. All the men deposited more muscle because they were exercising, and the steroids didn't add much. On the other hand, athletes don't take normal doses, and they are not looking for "statistically significant" effects. They often take huge doses, and a 1 percent improvement in performance can mean the difference between winning and losing. Huge doses of testosterone can increase muscle mass, as weight lifters have claimed for years.

Who Takes Steroids Now?

Use of anabolic steroids began with elite competitive athletes, but today it includes even high school students who are taking anabolic steroids for cosmetic purposes. Most researchers estimate that 3 to 5 percent of high school age athletes and 5 to 15 of adult athletes use performance-enhancing drugs (mainly anabolic steroids). The level of anabolic steroid use among young athletes exceeds use of any drugs other than alcohol, nicotine, or marijuana. Ironically, the introduction of testing has drastically reduced the incidence of anabolic steroid use in international elite competitions, although it still happens. Exact numbers are hard to come by because these athletes have also become better and better at escaping the detection, but they are clearly a small number (1% to 2% by some estimates).

How Anabolic Steroids Increase Muscle Size

Anabolic steroids do increase the size of muscle fibers. They do this by entering muscle cells and stimulating the production of proteins. However, strength increases less than muscle size because testosterone can cause fluid retention, which swells the muscles without making them stronger. For body builders this doesn't matter—as long as they are bigger, actual strength doesn't matter.

How well does increased muscle size translate to increased performance after anabolic steroid use? The jury is still out on this. The American College of Sports Medicine has stated that anabolic steroids can increase body mass, but they do not increase aerobic power or capacity for muscular exercise. In the end, we have to remember that research in this area is extremely controversial, and slight performance benefits in some situations mean the differences between winning and losing.

One mystery surrounding the claims that anabolic steroids increase muscle size is that the normal male body produces about as much testosterone as it can use. Doubling or tripling levels really shouldn't accomplish anything, and it doesn't. It takes amounts from ten to one hundred times normal values to get results. The hormone cortisol that breaks muscle down enters the picture here. Cortisol and testosterone are pretty similar to each other chemically. When tremendous excesses of testosterone are present, testosterone can actually bind to the cortisol receptors and keep cortisol from doing its normal job of breaking down protein. In this way, anabolic steroids may increase muscle mass in part by preventing the normal muscle breakdown by another hormone.

The Dangerous Side Effects of Anabolic Steroids

The huge amounts of anabolic steroids that athletes must take to get some benefit in muscle size present some very real risks to users. The first risk is simple to understand. Anabolic steroid use increases strains and tears of the tendons and ligaments connected to the muscle. These tissues are not as elastic as muscle, and it's possible that they just can't keep up with the abrupt increase in muscle size that the anabolic steroids cause. Up to 65 percent of the East German athletes who were given anabolic steroids during training experienced tightness or some other tendon/ligament problem.

Anabolic steroids can also change the profile of fats in the blood to a pattern that increases the risk of cardiovascular disease, and they can decrease sperm production and cause impotence. Finally, a growing number of individual cases indicate that direct damage to the heart muscle occurs in some users.

Special Risks for Women

Young women face special risks from anabolic steroid use because even small doses cause tremendous increases in their testosterone levels. Women's bodies have testosterone receptors, and they respond to the hormone if it is there. Naturally they make only about five percent of what men produce. Increasing that amount to levels comparable to normal males causes irreversible changes. The clitoris enlarges, as does the larynx, leading to a permanent deepening of the voice. Male-pattern baldness may also develop, other body hair coarsens, and some women develop bad acne. While these changes are mainly cosmetic, more dangerous changes also occur, such as the change in pattern of blood lipids that increases risk of cardiovascular disease. Women who use anabolic steroids lose the normal protection their gender provides against cardiovascular disease. Anabolic steroids also inhibit menstrual cycles and can lower libido (or increase it if the athlete just uses small doses).

Special Risks for Adolescents

Teenagers of either gender who have not finished growing face an additional risk if they take anabolic steroids. The rapid rise in testosterone in boys during puberty stimulates bone growth and so increases height, but it also will make bones stop growing. Testosterone both stimulates the normal rapid bone growth during puberty and, when it is done, triggers the end of this process. When teenage athletes take large doses of anabolic steroids, they can end up shorter than they would have been if they hadn't used anabolic steroids. We don't know yet what such large doses of anabolic steroids do to the reproductive system during puberty. This uncertainty is particularly troubling because so many high school students take these drugs.

Risks to the Reproductive System of Men

Normal adult men who take anabolic steroids don't suffer the irreversible effects described for women and adolescents. Nevertheless, there are bad health consequences. Effects on the reproductive system depend on how much the athlete takes. With small doses, libido may increase. High doses of anabolic steroids do the opposite: they "trick" the body into thinking that it is producing too much male hormone, and so the testes stop making testosterone and sperm, and the testes actually atrophy (shrink). These effects gradually reverse when steroid use is stopped. A certain percentage of each dose of certain anabolic steroids (testosterone itself and some of its precursors like androstenedione ["andro"]) is converted in the body to the female sex hormone estradiol. This can lead to the development of breast tissue—usually a pretty unpopular side effect.

The Heart and Circulatory System

High doses of anabolic steroids can enlarge the heart, thickening its walls to the point that the heart can't pump efficiently. This effect can reverse slowly after the athlete stops using steroids, but sometimes it doesn't.

Many cases of heart attacks in anabolic steroid users have also been reported. There are probably several reasons for this. Anabolic steroids decrease the levels of protective high density lipoproteins (HDL—"good cholesterol") and increase the low density lipoproteins (LDL—the "bad cholesterol") that increase risk of heart attacks. The normal effects of testosterone may be one reason that men are more vulnerable to heart attacks than premenopausal women. Estrogen and the absence of testosterone lead to a pattern of blood lipids that is higher in HDL and lower in LDL. Finally, anabolic steroids also increase the stickiness of blood cells called *platelets*. This clumping is one of the first steps in the formation of dangerous plaques inside blood vessels. Anabolic steroids increase the number of red blood cells, increase the factors in the blood that produce blood clots, and can increase blood pressure by causing fluid retention. Overall, they can place a big strain on the cardiovascular system.

What About Cancer?

Despite several high-profile cases like that of football player Lyle Alzedo, liver and brain cancer are not big concerns with anabolic steroids, but cancer of the reproductive organs *is* a concern. The reproductive organs are the most sensitive to testosterone-like hormones, and elevated levels of anabolic steroids may be a factor in the development of prostate and testicular cancer. Unfortunately, it's hard to know for sure if a treatment like anabolic steroids causes cancers that appear years after use. Sometimes it's just not possible to know what got the cancer-promoting process started.

Liver Disease

All the anabolic steroids that can be taken in pill form can cause several different liver diseases. These drugs most often cause a benign type of liver tumor that might go away when steroid use is stopped. However, occasionally these tumors are malignant and fatal. Anabolic steroids also sometimes cause a condition called *peliosis hepatitis* a condition in which normal liver tissue is replaced with blood-filled cysts. Sometimes these rupture and can cause a fatal hemorrhage.

"'Roid Rage" and Other Psychological Effects

No steroid effect has gained more press than the much-touted "'roid rage"—bouts of reportedly uncontrollable hostility and aggression that are said to be triggered by high doses of anabolic steroids. 'Roid rage has been blamed for many incidents of domestic violence associated with professional athletes in the last ten years. But is it real?

The idea that testosterone increases aggression came from some highly publicized studies that reported high testosterone levels in violent prison inmates compared to nonviolent inmates. These findings are controversial, as not every study has gotten such clear-cut findings. The association between aggression and testosterone is even weaker in men and women in the general population. On the other hand, numerous case reports have documented excessive aggression in athletes who are taking large doses of anabolic steroids. Research in animals tells a similar story. Showing that testosterone causes aggression in normal animals is difficult, but extreme excesses or deficiencies of testosterone do seem to influence aggression. For example, laboratory animals become less aggressive when their testes are removed, and aggression returns when the lost testosterone is restored. So even though the scientific literature does not provide a definitive answer to the question of whether anabolic steroids promote aggressiveness, it is reasonable to take seriously the self-reports of athletes who often note increased irritability and hostility.

Anabolic steroids have other psychological effects that are better documented. They can cause an increased sense of wellbeing, and at toxically high doses this can become *hypomania*—an elevation of mood and a need to be active that is pathological. Users like this state because they feel more energetic and happier.

The problem is that hypomanic people don't always make good or safe decisions, and in some cases this can cross over into an overtly psychotic, manic state. Furthermore, abrupt withdrawal of steroids can trigger a depressive episode.

Are Steroids Addictive?

Are anabolic steroids really addictive, in the way that cocaine and heroin are? There certainly has been a lot of media interest in this question, and the National Institute of Drug Abuse (NIDA) and the Drug Enforcement Agency (DEA) have classified them in this way. Scientifically, we don't really know whether this is true or not. Addictive drugs stimulate the "reward" system in the brain, and most scientists think that biochemical changes in the brain contribute to the compulsive pattern of drug taking that we describe as addiction. Steroids don't stimulate the reward system; however, steroid users clearly use compulsively, despite negative consequences. When a drug user loses control over use, and uses drugs despite the negative consequences, he has a problem, regardless of whether we would measure "addictive" changes in brain chemistry or not. Furthermore, steroid users often experience mood disorders or even depression that could be described as withdrawal when they stop. (However, from that perspective, pregnancy could be viewed as addictive, since an abrupt change in mood is associated with the equally huge endocrine changes at the end of pregnancy.) We are reluctant to describe anabolic steroids as addictive, but steroid use certainly has bad health consequences. And people certainly keep using steroids even though they understand these consequences, often because they are afraid of losing all the muscle mass that has been gained. So even if anabolic steroids don't stimulate the reward system in the way of drugs classically understood to be "addictive," people do use them in a compulsive and health-damaging way to avoid the reversal of their effects.

Major Dangerous Anabolic Side Effects in Adults

- Increased vulnerability to damage to tendons and cartilage

- Increased risk of cardiovascular disease: cardiac hypertrophy, altered blood lipids

- Increased fluid retention, blood pressure

- Increase or decrease in libido, decreased reproductive function

- Irritability, mania

- Reproductive tract cancer

Various Steroid Preparations

There are many different anabolic steroid preparations. All of them are both *anabolic* (muscle building) and *androgenic* (masculinizing). They differ from each other in several ways: (1) how they are given (by injection or in pill form), (2) how long they stay in the body, and (3) the tendency to be converted to the female sex hormone estradiol and so cause breast development and other feminizing qualities.

Testosterone must be injected because the liver degrades it so quickly that pill forms are not effective. If the molecule is changed slightly, it can be effective in pill form because it isn't so degraded by the liver. Unfortunately, this change also causes liver damage.

Many athletes are very sophisticated in their choice of anabolic steroids. One major goal of some athletes is to use drugs that tests can't detect. To achieve this goal, athletes often take long-lasting oral preparations during the early phases of training, then switch to testosterone itself before major competitions to allow the other compounds to disappear. The liver eliminates testosterone itself quickly, and once levels fall to near normal, tests can't tell the difference between testosterone produced by the testes and testosterone provided by pills.

Dose regimens that athletes use are often staggeringly high in conventional medical terms. Athletes often take anabolic steroids in "pyramids" of gradually increasing and then decreasing doses. They "stack," or combine, drugs and take doses that are often at least one hundred times greater than those needed to produce normal levels of testosterone. For example, one published regimen involves taking an oral anabolic steroid every day, adding testosterone injections every five days for about eight weeks. Then as the doses are decreased, human chorionic gonadotropin (hCG) or something similar is begun to allow the testes to start again. These regimens are repeated in "cycles" with breaks in between.

When athletes want to avoid the feminizing side effects of anabolic steroids like testosterone, they sometimes take drugs that block the actions of estrogen (like Tamoxifen) or drugs that prevent the conversion of testosterone to estrogen (like Testolactone [Teslac]). There are also drugs that can stimulate the atrophied testes to start producing sperm and testosterone again. Some athletes use these drugs to jump start their own systems after they stop an anabolic steroid "pyramid." Clearly this kind of drug use, and counteruse, can create a complicated set of effects. Since most people that end up going down this road do so without adequate medical supervision, the results can be dangerous.

The lists below show some common drugs in this category, including some of the brand names they're sold under. This is only a partial list of all possible anabolic steroids, and most European drugs are omitted.

Anabolic Steroids

Taken by Injection

Testosterone (Malogen, Malogex, Delatestryl, Testoject)

Testosterone cypionate (Depo-testosterone, Textex)

Testosterone enanthate (Delatestryl)

Nandrolone (Deca-Durabolin, Durabolin, Kabolin, Nandrobolic)

Taken by Mouth (Tendency for Liver Problems)

Oxandrololone (Anavar)

Oxymetholone (Anadrol, Anapolon 50, Androyd)

Fluoxymesterone (Halotestin, Ora-Testryl, Ultradren)

Methyltestosterone (Android, Estratest, Testred, Virilon)

Steroids That Can Be Converted to Estradiol and Cause Breast Development

Oxymetholone (Anadrol, Anapolon 50, Adroyd)

Testosterone (Malogen, Malogex, Delatestryl, Testoject)

Testosterone cypionate (Depo-testosterone, Textex)

Testosterone enanthate (Delatestryl)

Veterinary Steroids (Steroids Approved for Use in Animals)

Boldenone (Equipoise)

Trenbolone acetate (Finaplix)

Stanozolol (Winstrol, Stromba)

Drugs Not Approved for Marketing in the United States

Bolasterone (Vebonol)

Clostebol (Steranobol)

Dehydrochlormethyl-testosterone (Turinabol)

Dihydrotestosterone (Stanolone)

Mesterolone (Androviron, Proviron)—oral

Metandienone (Danabol, Dianabol)

Methenolone (Primobolan, Primonabol-Depot)—oral testosterone ester, not toxic to liver

Methandrostenolone (Dianabol)—oral

Norethandrolone (Nilevar)

Steroid Use Is Rampant in Schools

Elizabeth Crane

While people have become used to drug scandals in professional sports, the trickle-down effect of steroids tends not to be addressed. Elizabeth Crane discovers that steroids are getting ever more popular among teenagers who might want to increase their athletic ability or simply want to look better. She urges increased education to heighten students' awareness of the rampant crisis in middle and high schools around the country. Elizabeth Crane's writing interests include education, parenting, food, and Internet topics. She is a member of the American Society of Journalists and Authors.

Thanks to Major League Baseball, anabolic steroid use and abuse is once again in the news. In his State of the Union address this January [2005] President [George W.] Bush called for legislation against steroid abuse in professional sports (federal laws against steroid use have been in place since 1990). In April, a bill called the Drug Free Sports Act that would regulate steroid use in professional sports began wending its way through Congress. And in May, California passed a law that requires teen athletes and their parents to sign an anti-steroid pledge. The leap from tightening steroid controls on the pros to tightening steroid controls on the young shouldn't surprise anyone in the education community. Kids, especially athletes, are increasingly "on the juice," and lawmakers, parents and educators are worried.

Students Need to Learn About Steroids

"School systems are getting hammered with having to come up with rules," says Jon Almquist, Fairfax County Public

Elizabeth Crane, "Roid Rage: Districts' Latest Drug Problem Doesn't Involve Getting High, But Getting Stronger," *District Administration*, vol. 41, July 2005, pp. 32–37. Copyright 2005 Professional Media Group LLC. Reproduced by permission.

School Athletic Training Program Specialist and National Athletic Trainers Association Task Force Chair. Education about steroids is, he says, the only way to reach the greatest number of kids and stem the abuse. Detection and testing alone aren't going to cut it. The task force lobbied to get $15 million in federal funding for education as well as testing onto an expansion of the existing antisteroid law passed in 2004. But even getting that amount of money set aside, he says, is "like chipping away at an iceberg."

The National Institute on Drug Abuse funds the University of Michigan's Monitoring the Future project, an annual survey since 1975 of 50,000 high school students around the country. From 1998 to 1999, the number of 10th graders who admitted to using steroids jumped from two percent to closer to three percent, and the perceived risk of steroid use slipped from sixty-eight percent to sixty-two percent. In 2004, the number of high school seniors who report using steroids at least once is 3.4 percent. If you think of the hundreds of kids playing high school sports in any given district and then imagine that three or four out of every hundred, on average, have used steroids, there's cause for concern.

Steroid use and abuse has been around for a long time, even among high school students. Almquist remembers the last time there was a big flare-up of steroid abuse in high schools. It was in the mid-80s when, he says, there was the first increase of kids experimenting with steroid use. "Kids knew they couldn't get caught," says Almquist, "so they used them." At the time, the abuse was eradicated by a two-pronged attack: vigorous education about the possible side effects and long-term health concerns plus mandatory blood pressure checks before games and practices. Since the kids were made well aware that higher blood pressure—a sign that something, possibly digestible anabolic steroids, may be in their bodies— meant restricted participation, a phone call home, and possible suspension, they stopped using.

Supplements Create Gray Area

Now, says Almquist, kids are using for a variety of different reasons, and once again they have little fear of getting caught. "The supplements issue has boiled over everything," he says. Protein powder, ephedra, and other non-FDA-regulated "supplements" that may or may not contain steroids are readily available at stores like GNC. Kids who aren't athletes are experimenting and becoming what Almquist calls "mirror athletes," individuals who become so obsessed with their own looks that they spend hours in the gym gazing at their physique in the mirror instead of working out or playing a sport. Unlike drugs and alcohol, steroids aren't about getting high, having fun and partying; in this case they're about making yourself physically and therefore sexually attractive. For the kid who is truly an athlete and is in a position to be recruited for college-level sports, the pressure to "beef up" can be intense. In some cases, coaches and even parents could be encouraging the idea that in order to compete, an athlete has to be bigger, stronger and leaner. And that makes supplements and steroids look mighty tempting.

Damned If You Do

Steroids are ridiculously easy to obtain. Just like any other popular and quasi-illegal substance, you just have to know where to look. The Internet is stop No. 1; south of the border is second. Friends and even coaches will share recipes for bulking up and burning fat. And when the high-achieving sports superstars who are serving as role models for young athletes are "on the juice," who are parents and teachers to say that steroid use is wrong? Even the governor of California can go on television and admit that when he was a body builder he used steroids (they were legal then), and in the same breath tell kids not to take drugs.

To keep kids from trying steroids, says Carleton Kendric, family therapist and the author of *Take Out Your Nose Ring,*

Honey, We're Going to Grandma's, you have to hit them where they live. "Appeal to their vanity," he says. When talking to kids about smoking, showing them a blackened and diseased lung might gross them out but they aren't going to believe that could happen to them some time in the future. "You have to make it personal and immediate." The "you're going to die" approach doesn't work. Almquist agrees. "You shouldn't say to 16 year olds, 'you could die in a car accident if you drive too fast.' You say, 'you could lose your license and not be able to drive at all for two years.' That's an immediate and, to them, a more horrible consequence." When discussing steroids, once you tell kids that steroids can give them tiny testicles and "acne up the ying-yang," you've got their attention.

Damned If You Don't

The real problem with steroids, Kendric readily admits, is that they are effective. "All drugs are taken for one reason: they work. Steroids work so damn fast and so damn well it's almost like you can see the muscles growing from week to week. That's seductive." Boys are looking at models on magazine covers and saying, "I want to look like that," with six-pack abs and a well-muscled chest. They're using steroids to achieve sexual attractiveness. So are girls. In low doses, steroids can act as a diet drug, causing the body to lose fat, gain muscle, getting a girl "ready for bathing suit season" and again, enhancing her sex appeal. The look that girls are going for, either the "unnaturally thin with fake boobs that defy gravity look or the improbably tight, lean, toned, athletic look," they can achieve with steroids without the kind of discipline and effort it would take otherwise. "You get more of what a weight-trained athlete gets, fast. This stuff works." And in greater doses and in combination, it works even better. "If you become a little chemist and start stacking [using multiple drugs at higher dosages], the sky's the limit."

You can also, of course, crash and burn. "You can get very negative side-effects within weeks," Kendric says. It's important to be honest with teens—not everyone experiences negative side effects from steroids. "It is legitimate and honest to say you may be one of the ones without side effects. But you have to make it clear that it's like Russian roulette." One user could be lucky, while another could be covered in zits. What's in the steroids they're taking is unpredictable as well. Products purchased over the Internet can come from anywhere, can contain all kinds of fillers and unknown materials, and may not even contain the substance the user believes he or she has purchased. "People lie," says Kendric. "You don't know what is in what you're taking. We don't know what these drugs can do to you over your lifetime. You have to ask kids, 'Do you want to be part of a long-term guinea pig study?'"

Run for the Border

Mexican drugs are a lure to kids in the border states, especially in Texas, where high school sports are something of an industry. "It's worse for us here in the valley," says Chris Ardis, a high school teacher and weekly columnist in McAllen, Texas, a town in the Rio Grande valley. "You can go across the border to a pharmacia in fifteen to twenty minutes. It's that accessible." Ardis has had students tell her that the counter help in a Mexican pharmacy will offer to inject substances on the spot. While other drugs may merit just as much time and energy spent on education and prevention—the list of what teens can experiment with boggles the imagination—"the fact that even one kid committed suicide on steroids is enough to make it a concern."

Interestingly, economics plays a role in steroid use. Troy Mott, offensive coordinator for the Napa (Calif.) High School varsity football team, knows how easy it can look to get steroids over the Internet, but in reality, it's expensive. "Most kids don't have the means to buy cycles of steroids," he says. "We have way more problems with over-the-counter supplements." Kids shop at their local GNC for "supplements" that will supposedly help them grow bigger. "We steer them away from creatine and all that," says Mort, by talking to the kids about proper nutrition and the safest way to build muscle and lose fat. "Creatine is hard on the liver and kidney—that's not the way to be a good athlete."

Students Need to Know the Facts

Education is key to preventing kids from trying steroids in the first place. "An athletic trainer can tell you there's a health risk" with any steroid use, Almquist says, but engaging in risky behavior is often the hallmark of being a teenager. The medical community's recommendations, unfortunately, don't carry a lot of weight with kids, especially in this case. "Doctors tried to say, 'Steroids don't work,' when they clearly do," says Almquist. "Now they're saying, 'Steroids work but they're bad for you,' and kids won't listen." Coaches and athletic trainers have to learn from the "mistakes of the medical community" and emphasize that the health of the athlete comes first by laying out the facts:

- Used appropriately, steroids are a safe drug, just as opiates, when prescribed for pain by a doctor, are safe and effective.

- Anything used without control and in excess is bad for you.

- Steroid use is cheating. It gives an unfair advantage to some while leaving others out.

Proper training of coaches is a big first step, one that the national task force is working on. Laws need to be passed that make distribution of anabolic steroids illegal, and parents, teachers and students have to be educated on the risks and warning signs of steroid abuse.

The California Interscholastic Federation, the governing body of high school sports in California, has instituted a series of rules that any high school that wishes to stay in the CIF fold will have to follow. Barbara France, principal at Napa Valley High School in Napa, Calif., is happy that CIF is taking the lead in formalizing a steroid policy. Now, student athletes at Napa High and their parents are required to sign a piece of paper that specifically bans them from using steroids. "Having language in there specific to steroids gives our policy teeth," says France. "It gives us a platform to speak from" when dealing with the parents. There is no drug testing in place at Napa High; France doesn't see the need, and couldn't afford it anyway. Health education that contains a unit on steroids and close communication with the student body, she says, should do the trick. Coaches who may not have sufficient training in recognizing steroid use will be brought up to speed: beginning in 2008, CIF will require a coaches' training program that includes education on recognizing steroid abuse.

Healthy Dose of Self-Esteem

Kendric would like to see drug abuse discussed at an earlier age, since for him part of combating abuse is creating a healthy sense of self-esteem. "Some people want to be the star so badly," he says, "that they risk harming their body." As a society, we have a "passion for excelling and winning," says Almquist. "We created it, now we have to deal with it." Parents expect the school to step in to educate, stop steroid abuse, and create testing that will eradicate steroid users. But, Almquist says, parents are the first to object when it is their child caught using. "Kids get it. Kids like the rules to be enforced, but they don't always admit it." Laws against steroid use—state and federal laws are on their way—are a "good concept" because they force the issue, but the use of extreme punishments like a two-year suspension (proposed in some current legislation) could ruin lives, not save them.

"You have to define 'caught using steroids,'" Almquist says. What he can see happening is a situation where schools turn a blind eye to abuse because they can't afford the process of verifying and following through on the accusation. "If you are obligated to test you're also obligated to prove, so you never make an accusation because the process [of proving abuse] is so huge, cumbersome and expensive." Assuming that randomized testing and laws against steroid distribution are in place, Almquist recommends a policy that punishes first-time offenders without wrecking their careers. "Making mistakes is part of growing up; we have to expect kids to make mistakes." First offenders would receive a thirty-day suspension from sports and mandatory counseling. A second offense, however, would merit stiffer penalties. "Then you throw the book at them," says Almquist.

Education should focus on lifelong good health first rather than coming in after the fact to tell kids that what they may already be doing is bad for their health. "It is my hope," says Kendric, "that a fuller exploration of this complex issue develops."

For Ardis, teaching all members of the school community how to recognize steroid use is the key to stopping it. "They have the marijuana talk at our in-service every year," she says. "If there's one thing I know it's how to recognize marijuana use. I would hate to think that there is a child using steroids right under my nose and I wouldn't know."

Pros and Cons

Education about steroids and even mandatory testing isn't going to eradicate the problem if at higher levels of competition steroid use is condoned. Almquist asks rhetorically, "Do the pros have an influence? Darn right they do." Professional sports have a responsibility to make the ramifications of steroid use significant. "Major League Baseball's policy is a joke. The NFL's program is more effective." All the "I didn't do it" testimony on the news every night sends kids the wrong message as well. "Kids learn there's a way out of everything instead of learning to be responsible for their actions." They also know that certain drug screens catch only certain drugs; tests have to be made specific for steroids in order to be effective.

Maybe, slowly, things are changing. On May 12, [2005] Major League Baseball gave fifteen-game suspensions to eleven minor league players. All eleven tested positive for steroids. Giants manager Felipe Alou was quoted in the *San Francisco Chronicle* as saying, "I believe they should test kids when they sign. . . . If you test positive, we won't sign you. No million-dollar bonus." Maybe if the big boys start to play by the rules, the kids who admire them and want to be like them will, too.

Some Parents Facilitate Steroid Use

James Battaglio

Students are interested in taking steroids to enhance their perfor-mance or to sculpt their bodies. Yet, as James Battaglio finds, it is often the parents who push their children into steroid use. Ac-cording to the author, overly ambitious parents, influenced by the media and prospects of multimillion dollar pro contracts, of-ten undermine the integrity of high school and college sports. James Battaglio has spent the last forty years dividing his time between journalism and healthcare administration. His articles have resulted in numerous regional and national journalism awards.

I was prepared to hear that some of the jocks Robert Arciero sees in his UConn [University of Connecticut] medical practice are on steroids. I really was. After all, why should the privilege of bulking up and excelling in athletics be confined to professional sports? As the pros do, so too do their little brothers and sisters.

But 10-year-olds on 'roids and growth hormones? And some of them getting these from parents to boot? No way was I ready to hear that. I was practically dazed by the image of munchkin hulks power-lifting their little sisters before a vanity mirror while admiring their biceps and quads. "You can dis-miss that image," says Arciero, a doctor who specialized in or-thopedic knee, shoulder and sports medicine. "The ten-year-old girls using steroids are estimated at about three-and-a half percent, not much below the five percent of boys this age us-ing them."

New image: Little boys and girls power-lifting Mom and Dad. And if you think your sports-loving child isn't built like The Hulk and therefore you needn't worry about him or her experimenting with steroids, you could be wrong.

Steroid Use Is Easy to Disguise

The thing is, steroids need testosterone to give one the bulky, muscular look. But the drugs don't need testosterone to give a kid added strength and speed. That almost makes the situation worse—kids can be using steroids for quickness and power but still remain disguised from the telltale [famous body-builder] Charles Atlas look.

At the junior high level, when kids are entering puberty, they don't have the full complement of testosterone needed to shape muscles like those of the pros. The result is that they can get stronger, for sure, but it doesn't show as it does in an adult.

Things, as the good doctor points out, are "definitely getting out of hand."

And while some parents might ask how they can tell if their child is on steroids, others, perhaps desirous of having sired the next [basketball star] Michael Jordan or [golf pro] Tiger Woods, know full well where these drugs come from. They're the kids' suppliers.

Parents Push Steroids

Arciero said he's heard of parents looking for ergogenic aids (anything that makes one bigger, faster, stronger). Mostly, steroids are available through the traditional drug networks: gymnasiums, the street and foreign countries via the Internet. "It's just not that hard," says Arciero. "A 1999 study from West Virginia showed seven percent of all high school football players were current or former steroid users, and fifteen percent of them started taking the drug before age ten. In Minnesota the percentage of seventh graders queried showed nine percent had used steroids—five percent male and three and a half percent female—statistically making the percentage of users between boys and girls about the same. Sixth graders, seventh graders, high school kids . . . steroid use is rampant; it's like a street drug."

For the most part, doctors are finding that the kids who use steroids are the same kids prone to a higher usage of alcohol, tobacco and illicit drugs, almost as if there's a propensity to take drugs, regardless of what kind. That makes it sound as if just the bad kids are taking illegal performance enhancing drugs, right? Not so.

Everybody Wishes to Be the Best

A 1997 *Sports Illustrated* article by Michael Bamberger points out that in 1995, Olympic athletes were offered the following scenario: "If you were guaranteed to win and not get caught, would you use steroids?" Of 198 Olympians—the good, wholesome kids who supposedly represent the best of everything—only three said they wouldn't take the substance. Scarier yet: The same athletes were asked if they would take steroids if they could be guaranteed to win every competition for the next five years but would definitely die from them afterward. More than half said yes!

It gets worse. Studies taken both in the United States and Canada show that of the thousands of kids experimenting with steroids, a fair percentage are injecting themselves, and one-third of them share their needles with friends.

Further, only half the kids using these drugs think of them as bad.

"These kids and their families are influenced by multimillion-dollar athletes," says Arciero. "I see bizarre injuries outside the norm that make me suspicious, but I can't verify they're caused by steroid use because every kid denies it."

Bizarre Injuries

What's a "bizarre injury"? Doctors are seeing non-contact injuries whereby muscles have become too great a force, especially if there's an imbalance between muscles and hamstrings, thereby causing noncontact knee injures. The general suspicion here is that this person may be using steroids.

Bursts of speed create very troublesome injuries in kids who participate in strength training, even without steroids, but if you add steroids to the equation, it has a negative effect on tendons and ligaments by weakening them.

"It's a real paradox because you're doing it to get strong and this becomes counterproductive. Steroids add a double whammy. Now you have a strong muscle and a weak tendon. The result is bizarre, severe injury," says Arciero.

Okay, so what's the solution for those parents who aren't supplying their kids with these drugs and who *do* care about the injuries their young athletes may sustain if they fool with 'roids?

"I think it has to start at the education level. If you're going to talk about marijuana and cocaine, you need to throw steroids in there, too," says Arciero. "You've gotta get to them when they're young."

Sounds like first grade isn't too early.

CONTEMPORARY
ISSUES
COMPANION

CHAPTER 2

Steroids in Sports

Congressional Hearings Blast Steroid Use in Baseball

Dave Sheinin

This article chronicles the difficult hearings before a House committee investigating steroids in baseball. The author notes that the once seemingly untouchable heroes—Mark McGwire and Rafael Palmeiro among them—suddenly looked vulnerable. Their careers were stained and tainted, along with the sport of baseball, by allegations of steroid use. Dave Sheinin is a staff writer for the Washington Post.

On an extraordinary day of words and images, a House committee investigating steroids in baseball forced the sport to confront its past and rethink its future—encountering resistance on both counts—and the most extraordinary image of all was that of Mark McGwire, once the game's most celebrated slugger but now the face of the steroid scandal, reduced to a shrunken, lonely, evasive figure whose testimony brought him to the verge of tears.

During the course of an all-day, nationally televised hearing, the House Government Reform Committee fulfilled its goal of examining baseball's oft-criticized drug-testing program and its impact on steroid use among teenagers. Committee members said baseball's policy was full of holes and threatened to legislate tougher testing policies if the sport doesn't come up with them itself.

McGwire Stays Mum

In the process, however, the committee also ripped wide open the sport's most tender wound. Asked repeatedly by committee members whether he had used steroids in achieving unprecedented power numbers before his retirement in 2001, McGwire deflected each question—his non-answers standing in stark contrast to the unabashed frankness of Jose Canseco, McGwire's former Oakland Athletics teammate and an admitted steroid user.

While McGwire acknowledged "there has been a problem with steroid use in baseball," he responded to questions about his own involvement by saying, "I'm not here to discuss the past," or, "I'm here to be positive about this subject."

Baseball Under Public Pressure

The hearing came as baseball struggles to come to terms with what it admits is a steroid problem. In the past few months, leaked grand jury testimony by sluggers Jason Giambi and Barry Bonds showed them acknowledging steroid use and Canseco's book fingered some of the game's biggest stars as steroid users. Pressure from President [George W.] Bush and Sen. John McCain (R-Ariz.), among other national figures, forced baseball to strengthen its steroid policy this winter.

Rep. Thomas M. Davis III (R-Va.), the committee chairman, opened the hearing at 10 a.m. and brought it to a close more than eleven hours later. Throughout the day, the panel threatened congressional action to bring the sport's testing program closer in line to the Olympic testing program, which includes regular testing and swift, tough sanctions.

Committee members grilled baseball's leadership—Commissioner of Baseball Bud Selig, league officials Rob Manfred and Sandy Alderson, and union chief Donald Fehr—over what they saw as flaws in the sport's drug-testing policy, which was instituted for the 2003 season and strengthened this winter [2005] to include, for the first time, penalties for first-time offenders. However, baseball's current policy calls for a 10-day suspension for first offenses, as opposed to two years under the Olympics policy.

Selig, Fehr, and the other baseball officials implored committee members to understand their policy in the context of a collective-bargaining agreement in which items such as drug testing must be bargained.

The End of a Legend?

By the end of the hearing, the lawmakers seemed mostly unmoved by baseball's arguments.

"I have not been reassured one bit by the testimony I have heard today," said Rep. Stephen F. Lynch (D-Mass.). The testing program "has so many loopholes in this, it is just unbelievable." McGwire, whose Ruthian feats [accomplishments like those accomplished by Babe Ruth] on the field in the late 1990s made him a national folk hero, sat on the same panel but never made eye contact with Canseco, whose recent tell-all book gave voice to the long-rumored view that McGwire's accomplishments—along with those of many other contemporaries—were done with the help of steroids.

Steroids, Canseco said, were "as prevalent in . . . the late 1980s and 1990s as a cup of coffee." Canseco's audacious claims and admissions yesterday [date of articles is March 18, 2005] set him apart from the other players who appeared—McGwire, Baltimore Orioles stars Rafael Palmeiro and Sammy Sosa, and Boston Red Sox pitcher Curt Schilling. Schilling and the Chicago White Sox' Frank Thomas, who gave a statement via video conference, were invited because of outspoken views against steroid use. The others had all been connected to or accused of steroid use.

Players Have to Answer Tough Questions

Giambi had been excused from testifying because of his involvement in the grand jury inquiry into the Bay Area Laboratory Co-Operative (BALCO), a California nutritional supplements company, while Bonds was never invited to attend because, according to the committee's leaders, his presence would have overshadowed the substance of the hearing.

Palmeiro denied having used steroids, while Sosa—or his lawyers—crafted an opening statement in which he said he has never used "illegal performance-enhancing drugs," has never "injected myself or had anyone inject me with anything," and has not "broken the laws of the United States or the laws of the Dominican Republic."

"Let me start by telling you this," Palmeiro said in his opening statement, looking directly at Davis and pointing at the committee chairman with his index finger. "I have never used steroids, period."

McGwire's testimony, meantime, was noteworthy for what it did not say. "Asking me or any other player to answer questions about who took steroids in front of television cameras," he said, "will not solve the problem. . . . My lawyers have advised me that I cannot answer these questions without jeopardizing my friends, my family and myself. I intend to follow their advice."

Steroids Have Tainted Records

McGwire, who has been estimated to be 30 to 40 pounds lighter than at the end of his career, appeared on the verge of tears at least twice as he read his opening statement. The first time came as he referred to some of the participants of an earlier panel—the parents of two amateur baseball players whose suicides were attributed to steroid use.

The tone of the day was set by Sen. Jim Bunning (R-Ky.), whose previous career was as a Hall of Fame pitcher in the 1950s and 60s.

Apparently referring to modern sluggers like McGwire and Bonds, whose physiques expanded and whose home run totals began skyrocketing in their mid- to late-thirties, Bunning told the panel: "When I played with Henry Aaron, Willie Mays and Ted Williams, they didn't put on 40 pounds . . . and they didn't hit more home runs in their late thirties than they did in their late twenties. What's happening in baseball is not natural, and it's not right."

Bunning went a step beyond those who say the records of steroid-users should be marked by an asterisk, arguing that the records should be thrown out of the book. "If they started in 1992 or '93 illegally using steroids," Bunning said, "wipe all their records out. Take them away. They don't deserve them."

Locker Room Misinformation

William N. Taylor

Athletes inject themselves with steroids to gain an advantage over their competitors. In this selection, William N. Taylor tries to separate the myths—often perpetuated by athletes—and the science of steroid use. Taylor has been an anabolic steroid researcher for over two decades and served as physician crew chief for the United States Olympic Committee's Drug Control/ Education Program.

Most athletes who use anabolic steroids do so based on information obtained in locker rooms, underground "how to" anabolic steroid books, Internet sites, or by trial and error. Studies have shown that most, if not all, anabolic steroid users lack accurate information about the drugs they are using. This lack of knowledge is not surprising since, without a prescription, possession of anabolic steroids is illegal in the United States.

For decades, athletes and bodybuilders have utilized various methods and regimes in their anabolic steroid usage. All of these have contributed to the body of knowledge on which anabolic steroid users rely. Fellow users talk shop during workouts or when they socialize. They compare notes on which steroids to take, where to get them, how much to take, how long to take them, and so forth. Information obtained from the most muscular users and dealers is trusted over others, because this is the look other users want to achieve.

One can imagine how complex it becomes when many different anabolic steroids are used, and often they are combined with other drugs. There are simply too many variables and not enough scientific knowledge available to adequately describe such use. This, however, does not stop the "knowledge" about regimes that is shared by anabolic steroid users. . . .

None of the practices discussed in this chapter are meant as an endorsement. The information is provided solely to illustrate the informational gaps that exist between anabolic steroid users and the scientific community.

The First Cycle

The Anabolic Steroid User's Regime Most first-time anabolic steroid users begin with a single oral preparation. Based on information obtained from other more experienced users, they take anabolic steroid pills in moderate doses (two to five times greater than a clinically recommended dose) for six to eight weeks. Then the pills are discontinued for an equal amount of time in order to give their bodies a rest. Significant gains in muscle mass and strength are seen in users who have previously weight trained. When they compare this increase obtained with the use of anabolic steroids to the increase they experienced after a period of strength training, the results are dramatic. First-time anabolic steroid users usually experience a significant increase in muscle mass and strength and report psychological changes such as improved body image and increased self-esteem. At the very least, they conclude that anabolic steroids are harmless supplements.

During the period of anabolic steroid withdrawal, first-time users experience some loss of muscle mass and strength gains even though their workouts continue. Workout intensity and amount of weight lifted decreases. Minor injuries heal more slowly. Many experience some level of depression. They become impatient for the next cycle, and often cut short their rest periods.

The Science Behind the Regime Studies have shown that low to moderate supratherapeutic (larger than clinically prescribed) doses of anabolic steroids can significantly enhance muscle mass and strength in previously trained, otherwise healthy, athletes over and above the effects of weight training alone. The duration of anabolic steroid use in these studies varied from four to twenty-four weeks. Thus, scientific evidence supports significant muscle mass and strength gains with anabolic steroids during the first cycle. There is little scientific evidence to validate the user's practice of a rest phase for either safety or effectiveness of the next anabolic steroid cycle.

A recent study showed that after three months' cessation, much of the muscle mass and strength gains attained with anabolic steroid use remained. This study also reported that some of the biochemical abnormalities, including blood pressure, lipoprotein profiles, and liver enzymes, seen while on anabolic steroids return to normal range upon cessation.

The Second Cycle

The Anabolic Steroid User's Regime A second cycle is started because users are convinced that anabolic steroids have delivered the desired effects and will deliver desired effects again. They believe the same anabolic steroid taken at the same dose will again provide the same muscle mass increases.

Heavier anabolic steroid use begins when the second cycle gains are not as dramatic as the first cycle gains. In an effort to regain the dramatic increases experienced in the first cycle, they turn to experienced users who suggest more is better, longer is better, and other methods of administration are better. They begin to read black market anabolic steroid literature in search of the answer. Many users keep diaries, plotting their gains in an attempt to determine which, how, and what works best for them.

The Science Behind the Regime Anabolic steroid use causes an increase in levels and/or activity of liver and other tissue enzymes that degrade and convert the anabolic steroid into non-effective molecules. The enzymes tend to return to their normal level and activities when anabolic steroid use is discontinued. There is little or no scientific evidence to indicate that reintroducing a previously taken anabolic steroid, after a lengthy rest period, will cause an even greater induction of these enzymes to higher activity levels. It may occur, but it remains unproven.

Recent scientific studies have shown that anabolic steroid use causes a statistically significant increase in skeletal muscle cell numbers, muscle cell nuclei, and androgen receptors within these nuclei. A specific number of anabolic steroid molecules must bind to all of these receptors to optimize the stimulation of the genetic machinery. When the same anabolic steroid at the same dose is reintroduced, the steroid molecules are binding to more androgen receptors than they did previously. Thus, to continue significant increases in muscle mass and strength, a greater dose of the anabolic steroid may be required to activate the genetic machinery and manufacture new nuclei and androgen receptors to attain a higher level of protein synthesis again. Muscle mass has been shown to be tightly controlled by the quantity of the genetic machinery within skeletal muscle. It is likely that this mechanism is the reason that increases in the dose of anabolic steroids are required to extend muscle mass gains. However, this theory needs further investigation. Recent developments in scientific tools and modalities have made this a viable area for research and it is hoped that accurate information will be forthcoming.

The Third through Fifth Cycles

The Anabolic Steroid User's Regime By the third cycle, anabolic steroid users expand their use with regimes varying considerably. Availability of anabolic steroids, peer pressure, and inaccurate information accelerate their expanded use. Some users increase the dose of the same oral anabolic steroid previously taken. They may also take the higher dose schedule for a longer period of time. Other users begin a cycle with moderate doses, increase the weekly dose for several weeks, and then reduce the weekly dose for several weeks. This practice is called *pyramiding*. Athletes believe that pyramiding helps alleviate withdrawal symptoms. The muscle mass and strength gains associated with dose and duration increases are usually considerable. Rest periods usually become shorter.

Some users switch oral anabolic steroids, using steroid X for one cycle, steroid Y for the next cycle, back to steroid X again, and so on. This regimen is called *alternating cycles*. Alternating cycles are believed to help alleviate tolerance to a particular anabolic steroid. The muscle mass and strength gains are usually modest with this practice. Rest periods become shorter.

Other users take two or more oral anabolic steroids during a cycle. This practice is called *stacking*. Combining stacking and pyramiding is the practice called *stacking the pyramid*. Stacking the pyramid is believed to increase the effects of both anabolic steroids.

It is during the third cycle that some anabolic steroid users begin to experiment with injectable preparations. "You can't grow if you are afraid of the needle" is heard through locker rooms. Initially, another person administers the injectable preparation, but soon the user becomes a self-injector. Another practice is that of stacking oral and injectable anabolic steroids. This practice is believed to increase the total anabolic steroid concentrations and their effects on the body while reducing the toxic effects on the liver.

During the third cycle and beyond, users become more aware of the adverse side effects associated with anabolic steroid use. In an attempt to deal with adverse side effects, users often begin taking prescription drugs, with or without medical supervision, in an attempt to counter these effects. They can usually obtain these prescription drugs through black market steroid dealers.

The Science Behind the Regime ... Stacking multiple anabolic steroids together may have additive or synergistic influences on the total anabolic effects. However, there are no medical studies that have been conducted on humans to investigate these effects. The available scientific evidence to support stacking is derived from research conducted on livestock animals. The reader is reminded that these anabolic steroid regimes have little or no scientific support and more research is needed before definitive conclusions can be reached.

Beyond the Fifth Cycle

During this period, which may go on for years or decades, users continue many of the practices used in their previous cycles. Anabolic steroid doses escalate, more types are stacked, and self-injections of multiple anabolic steroids become common practices. Experimentation with other anabolic agents is the rule. Diaries are often abandoned as users realize that there are so many variables to their regimens that keeping workout records has become a worthless endeavor. Cycles become long periods of anabolic steroid use with little or no rest periods. In some users, rest periods become short periods of lower anabolic steroid use.

Abrupt withdrawal from heavy anabolic steroid use can have devastating consequences. Continued heavy anabolic steroid use can also have devastating consequences. Drugs believed to enhance the effects of anabolic steroids, and drugs used to treat the adverse effects from anabolic steroid use become common. Some of heavy users may be on a dozen or more various drugs at the same time.

Many heavy anabolic steroid users become anabolic steroid dealers in order to support their own habits. Heavy users experience physiological and psychological consequences. Many begin to realize their experimentation has become a biochemical and psychological nightmare with no end in sight.

The Blind Leading the Blind

Studies indicate that anabolic steroid users know more about the effects of the drugs than non-users, but limited knowledge is not enough. First-time anabolic steroid users enter into a type of drug use that seems safe enough to them, especially if they follow the patterns of use recommended by other users. They deny that any side effects will happen to *them*. They underestimate the addiction potential and withdrawal behaviors. They know little or nothing about the altered neurochemical effects. Over half of the first-time users will go into the fifth cycle and beyond with no real plans of quitting.

Many of the components of anabolic steroid use have been discussed. The applicable and available research that supports or refutes these components has also been presented. But, after all is said and done, the use of anabolic steroids is still not much more than a "blind leading the blind" proposition.

Without a prescription and medical supervision anabolic steroid use is both illegal and dangerous. The heavy anabolic steroid usage by over a million users during the 1980s and 1990s has had a plethora of both pesky, serious, and lethal medical health risks and consequences. . . .

The 1998 Homerun Race Led to Increased Steroid Use

Mark Fainaru-Wada and Lance Williams

Barry Bonds is arguably the best baseball player of his genera-tion. He has power, speed, and a great eye. The authors of this selection chronicle the homerun derby between Mark McGwire and Sammy Sosa and posit that the events of 1998 might have influenced Bonds to—allegedly—cross the line. Mark Fainaru-Wada and Lance Williams are investigative reporters for the San Francisco Chronicle *and have won many awards for their jour-nalistic work.*

On May 22, 1998, the San Francisco Giants arrived in St. Louis for a three-game series with the Cardinals. That weekend, Giants All-Star left fielder Barry Bonds got a first-hand look at the frenzied excitement surrounding Mark McG-wire, baseball's emerging Home Run King.

Bonds had recently remarried, but on this trip he was ac-companied by his girlfriend, Kimberly Bell, a slender, attrac-tive woman with long brown hair and green eyes whom he had met four years earlier in the players' parking lot at Candle-stick Park. Bell had been looking forward to the trip, and it was pleasant in many ways—a big hotel room with a view of St. Louis's famous arch; a wonderful seat eight rows behind home plate; and even tornado warnings, which were exotic to a California girl. But Bonds was sulky and brooding. A three-time winner of the National League Most Valuable Player award, he was one of the most prideful stars in baseball. All that weekend, though, he was overshadowed by McGwire.

Even by the standards of the modern game, the Cardinals' first baseman was a player of exceptional size and power. That summer the 6-foot-5 McGwire weighed 260 muscular pounds and was hitting balls that traveled in long, soaring arcs. The season was less than two months old, but he already had hit 20 home runs. McGwire's pace was ahead of Babe Ruth when he hit 60 home runs in 1927, and also ahead of Roger Maris when he hit 61 to break Ruth's record in 1961. Players, fans, and the media were already anticipating that McGwire could break baseball's most storied record, and the noisy attention he received as a result was impossible to ignore.

Before Friday night's game, even the Giants' coaches acted like fans gathering behind the batting cage and watching as McGwire hit 10 batting practice pitches into the stands. During the game itself, McGwire crushed a home run into an area of Busch Stadium's upper deck called "Big Mac Land." The home run entitled everyone in the sellout crowd of 43,000 to a free hamburger. For the Giants, Bonds went 1 for 4 with a double. The Cardinals won 4-3.

On Saturday night, McGwire singled in the first inning and scored from second when Bonds made a poor throw on a hit to left field. Then McGwire hit two more home runs, the second one bouncing off the Chevrolet sign on the left-field scoreboard. The Cards won 11-10.

On Sunday, Bonds himself hit a dramatic two-run homer, his 11th of the season, to tie the game in the ninth inning. But in the 12th, after the Giants had pulled ahead 6-4, McGwire hit an equally dramatic shot to tie the game again. It was his fourth home run of the series, and his 24th of the young season. The Giants finally won in 17, but Bonds's mood remained irretrievably foul.

On that trip, Bonds began making racial remarks about McGwire to Kimberly Bell. According to Bell, he would repeat them throughout the summer, as McGwire and Sammy Sosa, the buff, fan-friendly Chicago Cubs slugger who also was hitting home runs at an amazing rate, became the talk of the nation.

"They're just letting him do it because he's a white boy," Bonds said of McGwire and his chase of Maris's record. The pursuit by Sosa, a Latino player from the Dominican Republic, was entertaining but doomed, Bonds declared. As a matter of policy, "They'll never let him win," he said.

As he sometimes did when he was in a particularly bleak mood, Bonds was channeling racial attitudes picked up from his father, the former Giants star Bobby Bonds, and his godfather, the great Willie Mays, both African-American ballplayers who had experienced virulent racism while starting their professional careers in the Jim Crow South [the post–Civil War South where racists laws were in effect]. Barry Bonds himself had never seen anything remotely like that: He had grown up in an affluent white suburb on the San Francisco Peninsula, and his best boyhood friend, his first wife, and his present girlfriend all were white. When Bonds railed about McGwire, he didn't articulate who "they" were, or how the supposed conspiracy to rig the home run record was being carried out. But his brooding anger was real enough, and it continued throughout a year in which he batted .303, hit 37 home runs, made the All-Star team for the eighth time, and was almost completely ignored. For, as the 1998 season unfolded, the attention of all baseball focused on McGwire's home run chase and on his gentlemanly rivalry with Sosa. The quest to hit 61 home runs transfixed even casual fans, in the way that a great pennant race used to do in the old days.

Something about McGwire's appearances—the red hair and the freckled, craggy face that sometimes burst into a winning smile—seemed to invite affectionate hyperbole. The sportswriters who covered him wrote that McGwire had Popeye's forearms and shoulders as broad as Paul Bunyan's. The nature of his quest was also expressed in hyperbolic terms:

McGwire's home run chase was "a metaphor for the best in America," a newspaper editor told an Iowa professor who was studying the chase as a cultural phenomenon. It was more significant than "the ascent on Mount Everest," as San Francisco Giants marketing man Pat Gallagher proclaimed. And from acting baseball commissioner Bud Selig down to its ordinary fans—anybody who cared about the game and worried about its future—all agreed that McGwire's pursuit of the home run record was hugely important. It had made watching the sport of baseball enjoyable again, for the first time in quite a while.

Baseball's fans are among the most forgiving in all sports, but the toxic relations between team owners and the players union had put the fans' patience to the test for a generation. From 1971 through 1990, seven baseball seasons had been interrupted by labor disputes. The eighth interruption, which began in August 1994, lasted 234 days and led to the only cancellation of the World Series since World War I. It also nearly killed the game.

As always, both the union and the owners claimed the dispute was about baseball's future. Actually, it was just another fight about money. For fans, the dispute was dispiriting and pointless, an argument between millionaires and billionaires.

The owners finally reopened the ballparks, and the players slunk back into them two weeks after the 1995 season had been scheduled to start. In park after park they were greeted with a cascade of boos. Many fans just stayed away. Attendance in 1995 was down 28 percent, nearly 20 million, from 1993, the last pre-strike season. It crept back in the following seasons, but in 1997, attendance was still down 10 percent, or more than 7 million fans, from the pre-strike high. By some estimates the lockout had cost the owners $500 million in lost revenues in 1994, and $800 million more in 1995. More worrisome still were the many signs that interest in the game might have permanently ebbed.

Then, in 1998, McGwire's assault on Maris's record brought the fans back to baseball in droves. The Cardinals' home attendance, which had languished since the lockout, would top 3.1 million, a club record, and other National League clubs saw big gains as well. For fans, McGwire's escalating home run totals became a daily reminder of the game's underlying drama and intensity—and its history, for the ghosts of Ruth and Maris hovered about all summer long. And if McGwire's chase of the home run record evoked baseball's past, Sosa was a charming connection to its future, one of a stream of talented Latino players who were flooding into the game. Fans were drawn to Sosa, McGwire's friendly rival, and the complex ritual he went through each time he crossed home plate after a homer, including the blown kiss and the tap of his heart to honor his mother.

By mid-summer the home run chase took on a traveling circus atmosphere. One night in Phoenix, 25,000 people showed up to watch McGwire take his hacks in batting practice, while a TV station provided pitch-by-pitch commentary and the scoreboard registered the distance of each practice home run. A media pack worthy of a presidential candidate on election night tailed McGwire across the country, recording his every word and action.

In August, when McGwire had already hit 43 bombs, a veteran Associated Press writer named Steve Wilstein stopped by the big Cardinal's locker in Busch Stadium. As he waited for McGwire to emerge from the shower, Wilstein noted items in plain view on a locker shelf: a photo of McGwire with his 10-year-old son; a can of Popeye-brand spinach; a bottle of a product called androstenedione. Wilstein assumed it was some sort of vitamin.

But Andro was more than that. The product was a testosterone booster marketed by Patrick Arnold, a renegade chemist who was pioneering the development of steroids that would be undetectable by the most sophisticated laboratory tests. Andro was legal. But it had been banned by the International Olympic Committee, the National Collegiate Athletic Association, and the National Football League. Olympic doping experts told Wilstein that Andro had the same muscle-building effects as anabolic steroids, which Congress had outlawed in 1991. Andro was a steroid by another name. In the Olympics, using Andro was considered cheating. Users who got caught were banned.

Baseball, however, had no rules against steroid use, and a different attitude about cheating. From corking bats to doctoring balls to hiding a coach with binoculars in the scoreboard to steal signs, the impulse to cut corners was almost as old as the game itself. Players did what they could to get an edge, without shame or serious consequence. Performance-enhancing drugs had become another way to accomplish that. For decades, the game's drug of choice was not steroids but "greenies," or amphetamines, which were popped by players seeking to kick their performance up a notch, hoping to overcome fatigue, aches and pains, hangovers, even boredom.

Perhaps because of the sport's antipathy to weight lifting, steroids were slow to catch on. For much of the game's history, players were discouraged from pumping iron, lest they lose the flexibility and quick wrists needed to get around on the pitched ball.

That began to change in the mid-to-late 1980s. By his own account, the Typhoid Mary of steroid use in the big leagues was the Cuban slugger Jose Canseco, the first player to hit 40 home runs and steal 40 bases in the same season. Canseco was also McGwire's teammate on the dominating Oakland Athletics clubs of the 1980s. In 2005, out of baseball, financially strapped, and on probation for assault, Canseco would write a confessional memoir, claiming to have "single-handedly changed the game of baseball" by popularizing weight training and performance-enhancing drugs. Canseco said his own career proved that strength conditioning, when combined with steroids and human growth hormone, translated into a higher batting average and more power. He claimed that the drugs could transform a good player into a great one. After his Rookie of the Year season in 1985, when he hit 33 home runs, Canseco claimed other players began to emulate him, and weight training and juicing swept the game.

In the book's most enduring image, Canseco described going into the bathroom at the Oakland Coliseum with McGwire before A's games. There, he wrote, the two sluggers would inject themselves with the steroid Deca-Durabolin, then take the field.

But in 1998, Canseco's disclosures about his famous teammate were far in the unanticipated future. And in 1998, McGwire had been caught only with Andro, not with Growth or Deca. Still, the AP's revelation that McGwire was using a drug that would have gotten him banned from the Olympic Games pushed its way into the headlines. Many in baseball's establishment reacted with outrage—not at McGwire, but at Wilstein, the writer who broke the story.

Leading the attack was Tony LaRussa, the Cardinals' tightly wound manager. He lashed out at the media, agitating to ban the Associated Press from the Cards' clubhouse on the spurious grounds that Wilstein had violated an unwritten baseball rule by looking in McGwire's locker.

Acting commissioner Bud Selig promised baseball would commission a scientific study about the health effects of performance-enhancing drugs. But he made it clear he would take no action regarding McGwire and Andro.

Selig's deepest fear was that the Andro story would develop into a scandal that would ruin McGwire and kill baseball's lucrative renaissance just as it was beginning. Fans loved the long ball; crowds were packing the parks; the rancor of the strike was being forgotten; McGwire and Sosa were bringing baseball back from oblivion's edge. And if it sometimes seemed that baseball was devolving into an arcade game, with double-digit scores resembling those in football, and if players were showing up at spring training 15 pounds heavier and displaying the physiques of bodybuilders, those were concerns for another time.

Soon, the Andro story faded. Stubborn pitchers continued to challenge McGwire, and he continued to drive the ball. The rate at which he hit homers was unprecedented—once every 7.27 at bats, far above Ruth's career average of 11.76—and the distances they traveled inspired awe. At Busch Stadium, where the center field fence was 402 feet from home plate, he hit a 545-foot shot that slammed into a seat in the second deck. The club marked the spot by painting a big picture of a Band-Aid there. A home run in the thin air of Denver sailed out of Coors Field, bounced through the players' parking lot, and finally came to rest against a fence 700 feet from the plate.

McGwire hit number 62 on September 8 [1998] in St. Louis, amidst a wild celebration and before a national TV audience, and then continued hitting bombs: five of them in his final 11 at-bats, including two on the last day of the season, to finish with 70, four ahead of Sosa. In 36 seasons, no baseball player had topped the 61 home run mark—and now two players had blown past it in the same year. Many at the time said McGwire's 1998 season was the greatest offensive performance in the history of the sport.

On the West Coast, Barry Bonds was astounded and aggrieved by the outpouring of hero worship for McGwire, a hitter whom he regarded as obviously inferior to himself. Bonds was 33 years old, had played in the big leagues for 12 years, and was known for an unusual combination of speed and power. In 1993, when he joined the Giants, Bonds had signed what was then the richest contract in the game: $43.75 million for six years. In 1996 he had become the second player in history, after Canseco, to hit 40 home runs and steal 40 bases in the same season. Bonds knew he was on his way to the Hall of Fame. For as long as he had played baseball, Bonds had regarded himself as better than every other player he encountered, and he almost always was right.

But as the 1998 season ended, Bonds's elite status had slipped a notch. The game and its fans were less interested in the complete player who could hit for average and power, and who had great speed and an excellent glove. The emphasis was shifting to pure slugging. From now on, the biggest contracts and the most adulation would go to big, muscular players who could put up home run numbers unlike anything the game had ever seen: players like Mark McGwire. As McGwire's pursuit of the home run record became the constant topic of the nation's media, and as McGwire was celebrated as the best slugger of the modern era and perhaps the greatest slugger who had ever lived, Bonds became more jealous than people who knew him well had ever seen.

To Bonds, it was a joke. He had been around enough gyms to recognize that McGwire was a juicer. Bonds himself had never used anything more performance enhancing than a protein shake from the health-food store. But as the 1998 season unfolded, and as he watched Mark McGwire take over the game—his game—Barry Bonds decided that he, too, would begin using what he called "the sh—."

Bodybuilding and Steroids

Steve Sailer

In this viewpoint, Steve Sailer explores the bodybuilding past of California governor Arnold Schwarzenegger and argues that his image sends all the wrong messages to the people who admire him for his savvy and movie-star career. Steve Sailer is president of the Human Biodiversity Institute. He is a columnist for VDARE.com and the film critic for The American Conservative *magazine.*

No man owes more to steroids and steroids owe more to no man. . . .

The Austrian-born superstar began his bodybuilding career in the late 1960s, an era when extreme muscularity in a man was considered something only the lower class admired. Despite his inability to speak English other than in a thickly accented monotone, by the late 1980's he had made himself the biggest movie star in Hollywood. In the process, he redefined masculinity in his own bulging, brutalitarian image. . . .

In his 1977 autobiography, *Arnold: The Education of a Bodybuilder,* he wrote, "I knew I was a winner. I knew I was destined for great things. People will say that kind of thinking is totally immodest. I agree. Modesty is not a word that applies to me in any way." Way back in 1984, the author of a *Rolling Stone* magazine story on Schwarzenegger's extraordinary life felt obligated to include a section explaining that Schwarzenegger, not having been born an American, was ineligible to become president. As for being the son of a man who was a Nazi before Arnold was born in 1947, the sins of the father have not been widely considered the responsibility of the son for a few thousand years.

The 'Bad Boy' of Politics

Al Gore's admission that he smoked marijuana didn't keep him from winning the popular vote in 2000. Nor does it seem likely that Schwarzenegger was ever much of a pothead. In Quentin Tarantino's *Jackie Brown*, Samuel L. Jackson comes home to find Bridget Fonda smoking dope on the couch. He points out, "That (stuff)'ll rob you of your ambitions." She replies, "Not if your ambition is to get high and watch TV." If Schwarzenegger had more ambition than he has now, he'd have to be running for Galactic Overlord.

When Schwarzenegger was thinking of trying for governor in the 2002 election, political consultant Gary South, the eminence grise (from the French expression, meaning "grey eminence", powerful advisor) behind Gray Davis, faxed a *Premiere Magazine* article to hundreds of journalists containing allegations that Schwarzenegger pawed women and cheated on his wife, Maria Shriver. Whether Californians, who tended to strongly support Bill Clinton in his 1998 scandals, will be shocked by such claims about a movie star is questionable.

Steroids Made Him a Star

The one aspect of the star's background that's getting the least attention, however, might be the one that most deserves inquiry: anabolic steroids. Elvis Costello claimed, "There's no such thing as an original sin," and that's certainly true for a politician having a bad dad, smoking dope, or chasing women. But the unique case of Arnold Schwarzenegger and his relationship with the manly molecules he injected is an exception.

The masculinizing effects of steroids on his massive muscles, deep voice and incredibly assured attitude have contributed to the male charisma that has made him the highest salary movie star ever ($30 million for *Terminator 3*). . . . In turn, his body and his career have provided steroids with their best advertising.

Schwarzenegger doesn't like talking about steroids, but he doesn't deny using them. He has seldom been quoted on the record about them without putting some mitigating spin on his admission, an example of the verbal caginess that should serve him well in politics. For example, in a mail order pamphlet he wrote in 1977 entitled *Arnold: Developing a Mr. Universe Physique*, Schwarzenegger claimed, "Yes, I have used them, but no, they didn't make me what I am. Anabolic steroids were helpful to me in maintaining muscle size while on a strict diet in preparation for a contest."

A 1992 interview in *U.S. News & World Report* read, "On his steroid use: 'In those days you didn't have to deal with the black market. You could go to your physician and just say, 'Listen, I want to gain some weight, and I want to take something.' Then the physician would say, 'Do it six weeks before the competition, then it will be safe.' And that's what you would do. The dosage that was taken then vs. what is taken now is not even ten percent. It's probably five percent."

A Poster Child for Steroid Use

Schwarzenegger didn't publicly argue for steroid use the way Timothy Leary spoke out for LSD (and Schwarzenegger denounces the drugs in the 1999 edition of his 832-page *The New Encyclopedia of Bodybuilding*). Still, Schwarzenegger promoted his only-possible-with-steroids body and personality more aggressively than anyone ever.

Reporters usually refer to his "using steroids as a bodybuilder in the 1970s," but he probably began some time before then. The former Mr. Austria Kurt Marnul became the young prodigy's weight-training mentor in 1961 when he was fourteen.

According to Nigel Andrews' unauthorized biography *True Myths: The Life and Times of Arnold Schwarzenegger*, at some point "Marnul introduced Arnold to steroids, which were then legal. In the early 1960s, the trainer claims, 'There was no weightlifter in the world who did not take them. You could get prescriptions for them from the doctor. Arnold never took them, though, without my supervision.'"

Muscle Made for the Movies

Schwarzenegger won the Mr. Olympia title six times in a row from 1970–1975, then retired from competition and made a couple of films. He made a comeback in 1980 and won again, then moved into movie stardom with 1982's *Conan the Barbarian* and other roles that required spectacular muscularity.

In his defense, Schwarzenegger might well have won without steroids if nobody else used them either. But he wouldn't have looked as formidable for his leap into movies.

His publicist Pat Kingsley said, "Arnold hasn't done steroids since they were made illegal." (Congress made them a controlled substance in 1990, shortly before George H.W. Bush bizarrely nominated Schwarzenegger to be the chairman of the President's Council on Physical Fitness.) Indeed, he seemed smaller for some of his recent roles.

Schwarzenegger has a nude scene in this summer's *Terminator 3*, however, and he's in amazing shape for a man who recently turned fifty-six. He denied using a body double, saying, "I went into the mode of training as if I'm preparing for a competition again."

Anabolic steroids, artificial male hormones designed to build muscle, aren't the worst problem drug bedeviling our society, but they are abused, with lamentable health and behavioral consequences. According to the National Institute on Drug Abuse, about five percent of male 10th graders have used anabolic steroids, some for athletics, but many just for cosmetic purposes.

Setting a Bad Example

NIDA reports, "Anabolic steroid abuse has been associated with a wide range of adverse side effects ranging from some that are physically unattractive, such as acne and breast development in men, to others that are life threatening, such as heart attacks and liver cancer. Most are reversible if the abuser stops taking the drugs, but some are permanent."

Some users are prone to what bodybuilders call "'roid rage." In 1984, Oxford graduate Sam Fussell, the timid six-foot, four-inch, 170-pound scion of a family of literary critics, read Schwarzenegger's autobiography. As described in Fussell's book *Muscle: Confessions of an Unlikely Bodybuilder*, he immediately began a four-year devotion to bodybuilding that led Fussell to quit his job in publishing and move to Southern California with little besides his Schwarzenegger poster and books. There, with the help of massive doses of steroids, he topped out at 259 pounds of muscle. "From my first moment on the juice, nothing else mattered. Nothing but my workouts, my growth, my meals, my injections. . . ."

Fussell wrote, "The reaction wasn't just physical. I found myself psychologically affected as well . . . I needed to rule . . . I was fueled by my own anger, which I seemed to draw from an inexhaustible source. I watched almost as a spectator as my body operated beyond my control. I wasn't just aching for a fistfight, I was begging for it. I longed for the release. So I strutted through the city streets, a juggernaut in a do-rag, glaring and menacing anyone who met my eye. . . . The shouting matches invariably ended as soon as I discarded my shirt for battle. My opponents always fled."

Schwarzenegger's impact on most young men was far less overwhelming. Still, it's hard to fully dismiss the notion that it's increasingly Arnold's world and we're all just living in it.

A Ballplayer's Death
Is Linked to Steroids

Mark Fainaru-Wada

In this essay, Mark Fainaru-Wada recounts Rob Garibaldi's story, the story of a high school and college baseball player who did not want anything more than to make it to the major leagues. Consumed by his wish to turn pro, Garibaldi—who felt he was too small and light—turned to steroids early and went far beyond what seemed reasonable. He developed severe psychological problems, was thrown off the team, and finally killed himself. Mark Fainaru-Wada is an award-winning reporter for the San Francisco Chronicle.

For years, the message had been clear to Rob Garibaldi, a kid with major league tools but minor league size: get bigger. Fast.

Garibaldi heard it from the coach/nutritional supplement salesman who started him on legal weight-gaining substances at age sixteen.

He heard it from University of Southern California trainers who handed him two shopping bags of supplements on a recruiting visit and told him he needed to put on twenty pounds.

He heard it from pro scouts who said he just didn't quite fit the physical profile they were looking for in big league baseball.

Garibaldi's response was to use steroids, and his parents and his psychiatrist say it was the extensive use of those drugs that led the once-vibrant young man down an increasingly troubled path that ended in a derailed baseball career, depres-

Mark Fainaru-Wada, "Dreams, Steroids, Death—A Ballplayer's Downfall," *San Francisco Chronicle*, December 19, 2004. Copyright © 2004 by San Francisco Chronicle. Republished with permission of San Francisco Chronicle and Copyright Clearance Center, Inc.

sion, and months of emotional turmoil before he ultimately committed suicide at the age of twenty-four.

Following His Role Models

His friends and family say Garibaldi, a former star high school outfielder in Petaluma, was simply following behavior he was seeing everywhere—from the college ball fields where he competed to professional stadiums where superstars like Barry Bonds and Mark McGwire clouted home runs regularly.

His father, Ray Garibaldi, says he learned of his son's steroid use just months before Rob shot himself. He confronted Rob and demanded to know what drugs he was using. The son erupted, choking his father and yelling:

"I'm on steroids, what do you think? Who do you think I am? I'm a baseball player, baseball players take steroids. How do you think Bonds hits all his home runs? How do you think all these guys do all this stuff? You think they do it from just working out normal?"

His mother, Denise Garibaldi, said she heard the same kinds of explanations.

"In his mind, he felt like all the guys were getting away with this," she said. "Cheating and doing this is part of what's going on every day, and it was required. This was what you had to do to be a ballplayer.

"He said that in order to make it into that caliber, you had to do steroids. And if Barry Bonds is doing it, Mark McGwire was doing it, then skinny little old him for sure had to be doing it."

The Garibaldis said Bonds was one of Rob's idols growing up, and Denise, a clinical psychologist, believed that was a factor. "As far as he was concerned, Bonds gave him permission to use," she said.

A Public Health Issue

As all this was unfolding in the Garibaldi household, federal authorities in the Bay Area were launching an investigation that would ultimately result in indictments involving the distribution of steroids and other performance-enhancing drugs to some of the world's greatest athletes—and turn public attention to the influence that drug cheating by sports stars might have on the nation's youth.

The *Chronicle* reported this month [December 2004] on the grand jury testimony of two baseball stars who were among the most prominent clients of BALCO, the Burlingame laboratory at the center of the sports doping scandal.

Bonds, who set baseball's single season home run record with seventy-three in 2001 and has publicly denied using steroids, told the grand jury that he used a clear substance and a cream provided by a friend who is now accused of distributing BALCO drugs, but that he never thought they were steroids. New York Yankees slugger Jason Giambi testified that he used steroids and also injected human growth hormone.

After the *Chronicle* reported on the testimony, U.S. Surgeon General Richard Carmona told the Associated Press that the problem of steroid use was "less a moral and ethical issue than it is a public health issue. If youngsters are seeing their role models practicing this kind of behavior and it seems acceptable, then we need to do something about that because it is a health risk."

Psychological Impact

In the early morning of October 1, 2002, sitting in a car just around the block from his parents' home, Rob Garibaldi finally put an end to what had been a tumultuous period plagued by depression, rage, and delusional behavior, using a .357 Magnum he had stolen the day before.

For a year and a half, the Garibaldis grieved privately, trying to make sense of their son's dramatic downward spiral. Then, in early March of this year [2004], they saw the parents of a Texas high school baseball player named Taylor Hooton describing on national television how their son had hanged himself as a result of steroid use. The Garibaldis found it hauntingly familiar, and soon began to tell Rob's story to high school students, national television audiences, and state legislators who had taken up the cause in the wake of the BALCO scandal.

An Early Problem

As the Garibaldis now realize, Rob's steroid use dated all the way back to the summer of 1997, when he was eighteen years old and had just been honored as a prep All-American at Casa Grande High School. That places him in a population of steroid users for whom parents, lawmakers, coaches, and experts are most concerned: teenagers.

An annual study by the University of Michigan indicates that steroid use among all students in eighth through twelfth grades rose yearly throughout the 1990s, an indication that many kids recognized the drugs could benefit not only athletes but boys and girls simply seeking the body beautiful.

Dr. Harrison Pope, the director of the biological psychiatry laboratory at McLean Hospital/Harvard Medical School, said in a telephone interview that in addition to the aggressive behavior often linked with steroid use, the withdrawal from using can lead to depression and, in extreme cases, suicide.

Legal and Illegal Drug Use

Garibaldi's concerns about his body and the use of steroids weren't the only issues he struggled with. Since age twenty-two, he had been taking antidepressants that have since been said to increase suicidal tendencies in children. He also had a learning disability that led him to take Provigil, a drug prescribed to help cope with the effects of attention deficit hyperactivity disorder. And there were periods of marijuana use and drinking that coincided with his taking some of the drugs, friends and family members say.

He also told his psychiatrist he was adjusting his prescribed medications on his own so as not to decrease the effects of the steroids.

Still, Garibaldi's psychiatrist, Dr. Brent Cox, said a series of rage incidents and other emotional issues coincided precisely with three separate, ten-week periods of steroid use that Garibaldi described during sessions. Similarly, excessive bouts of depression fell in line with periods when he had stopped using the drugs, Cox said.

Ray and Denise Garibaldi said their own extensive research convinced them steroids were the ultimate culprit in Rob's emotional demise.

Steroid Use Changed Him

Garibaldi went from being a young man universally described as outgoing and well adjusted to an entirely foreign figure to his friends and family.

"The behavior seemed to come back pretty reliably when he was using anabolic steroids and disappear when he stopped," said Cox, the psychiatrist, who spoke with the family's permission. "There was really a dramatic transformation in this guy. There was a really edgy, irritable quality when he was using steroids, like he was just ready to jump across the room and throttle you."

The Artificial Path

Rob Garibaldi's biggest problem was that he was too little. So he ultimately set out to bulk up in a way that all the weight lifting and nutritional supplementation couldn't help.

"This wasn't an adolescent kid who was looking for beach muscle or whatnot," said P.J. Poiani, who was one of Garibaldi's closest high school friends and who said he was with him when he took steroids for the first time. "This was a kid who every hope and dream he had was surrounded by baseball. And you do whatever it takes."

He was never going to be big enough—not like his father, a bear of a man who said he was a pretty good baseball player before an injury shortened his playing days, or his older brother Ray Jr., now six-foot-two and 200 pounds. From the time he was a five-foot-nine, 125-pound sophomore playing on Casa Grande's varsity squad, Rob had been trying to pump up.

It was then that Garibaldi began to lift weights and receive nutritional supplements, first from Rob Bruno, a salesman at a supplement company who coached Garibaldi on a traveling all-star team, and later from Casa Grande assistant coach Paul Maytorena.

When he left high school in 1997, after three years of lifting weights and ingesting an array of weight- and muscle-gaining supplements that included some legal but controversial substances, Rob was five-foot-eleven, 150 pounds—bigger, but not nearly big enough, he felt.

The Supplement Business

The supplements he took, his father said, included creatine and androstenedione, known as Andro, the steroid precursor Mark McGwire admitted to using when he hit seventy home runs in 1998. Creatine had become a popular supplement among athletes and gym rats, although there were warnings about its potential dangers, including possible cancer risks.

"What I say now and what I hope I said then is that you need to get stronger, not bigger," said Maytorena, who said he has a degree in exercise science from Sonoma State. Maytorena said he monitored Garibaldi's use of the supplements and provided his parents with information about the substances.

Bruno, who said he was a power-lifter for years, said he gave Garibaldi only a basic weight-gaining supplement distributed by his company and not creatine, but Ray Garibaldi said his son did receive creatine from the coach.

"Obviously, we're going to tell a kid what they need to do in regard to getting bigger and stronger," said Bruno. He said he told Garibaldi what he told many other youngsters, to use supplements as a complement to a solid weight-training program because, "If you're going to be a great athlete, you need to be strong."

Garibaldi later would tell his parents that taking steroids was essentially an extension of taking these supplements.

Crossing the Border

In the summer after Garibaldi's high school graduation, in preparation for beginning school and a baseball career at the College of San Mateo, Garibaldi decided he needed some artificial assistance with his weight-training program.

"He called me up one day and said he wanted to get bigger, wanted to get stronger," said Brian Seibel, one of Garibaldi's closest friends. "He thought steroids were the way to do it."

Garibaldi had heard Mexico was an easy place to buy steroids—which are illegal to buy or use without a doctor's prescription—so he and Seibel told their respective parents they were going camping, hopped in Garibaldi's car, and headed south. They stopped in San Diego, slept in the car overnight, then drove into Tijuana the next morning.

Seibel thinks Garibaldi knew going in that he wanted to get Sustanon, a substance the Web site steroid.com describes as a "very popular steroid" that is a "mixture of four different testosterones which, based on the well-timed composition, have a synergistic effect." The teenagers walked into the first pharmacy they came upon, and Garibaldi was directed to a doctor's office around the corner. There, he gave the doctor some cash, Seibel said, then returned with a prescription.

Garibaldi hid the steroids behind a car stereo speaker as he and Seibel drove back across the border.

"We were in Mexico I would say probably even less than an hour," recalled Seibel, who said he only went along for the trip and never had any interest in using steroids.

The whole transaction cost about $250 to $300.

The Cycles of Steroid Use

Athletes typically take steroids for a period of weeks, called a cycle; upon returning home, Garibaldi began his first cycle. The stuff from Mexico, Poiani said, had everything he needed—syringes, needles, and steroids—and so, with Poiani watching, Garibaldi injected himself in the buttocks for the first of what would be many times.

"I mean, Rob always talked about how he was scared of needles in terms of the doctor, so it was kind of comical in some ways," Poiani said. "He was kind of laughing about just how scared he was, but he just did it. And then it got easier."

Garibaldi completed an eight-week cycle that summer, according to Poiani, and the results showed. Poiani thought his pal gained eight to ten pounds.

Spiraling Out of Control

Garibaldi eventually abandoned his plan to attend and play ball at San Mateo. Instead, he lived at home most of that first year out of high school and helped his old high school coach, Bob Leslie, who had mouth cancer and would die that June.

At that same time, Poiani said, Garibaldi was working out a lot—and taking another cycle of Sustanon.

"He took a *long* cycle," Poiani said. "Because I remember at the time being a friend thinking, 'What the hell are you doing?' I think people usually take six- to ten-week cycles. I think he was into something like fourteen weeks or something crazy."

Cycles are designed to optimize the effectiveness of the drugs and minimize side effects, with users being "on" for a number of weeks and then "off" for a similar period of time.

"He blew up at that point, I mean for his standards," Poiani said.

One year later, after enrolling at Santa Rosa Junior College in the fall of 1998, the now-five-foot-eleven, 165-pound Garibaldi put together one of the most prolific seasons in school history. He hit .459 with fourteen home runs and seventy-seven runs batted in, earning him state Community College Player of the Year honors.

A College Scholarship

The performance was good enough to earn him a scholarship to USC [University of Southern California], which had one of the nation's top Division I baseball programs. It was also good enough to get Garibaldi selected by the New York Yankees during the June 1999 major league draft, though not until the forty-first round.

"They have their body types and all that," Garibaldi told the *Press Democrat* of Santa Rosa. "I'm not quite big enough."

Garibaldi chose the scholarship to USC, the top college choice of his parents, who were particularly comforted by the school's strong program to help kids with learning disabilities. During a recruiting visit to USC in October, while Ray and Denise met with an academic counselor, Rob took a tour of the training facilities.

He emerged loaded down with containers of supplements, including creatine.

"They said I have to put on twenty pounds," Rob, who had just turned twenty-two, told his parents.

Early Successes

Garibaldi started at USC in January 2000, and he immediately had an impact. He hit .329 with eight home runs and forty-four runs batted in to help the Trojans reach the College World Series. *Baseball America* placed him among the top one hundred college players going into the 2001 season.

"When they went to the World Series, he said, 'All of my dreams have come true,'" his mother recalled. "Being on that field meant everything to him. It was right after that that it all went askew."

Losing Control at USC

First came news that Garibaldi was having academic troubles.

So rather than spend the summer playing ball in the Cape Cod League, as planned, he returned home and took classes to ensure he would be eligible the next season. He became depressed, mostly because of the academic struggles, girlfriend troubles, and the transition from the high of the College World Series to the low of not even being able to play ball at all. His mom suggested he see Cox, a psychiatrist colleague of hers.

Cox ultimately prescribed the antidepressant Effexor, and the drug seemed to work well. Not long before returning to USC, Garibaldi told Cox his time back home represented "the best summer I ever had," according to the psychiatrist's records. Cox knew nothing about his steroid use.

The Troubles Increase

In September, Garibaldi began a ten-week cycle of Deca Durabolin, which steroid.com describes as "the most widespread and most commonly used injectable steroid." His parents visited USC one month later, and Denise said Rob pulled her aside at one point to show her how he had taken a baseball bat to his dresser.

Garibaldi told his mom he was in trouble: he had failed a midterm, was sleeping excessively, and wasn't really sure the antidepressants were helping at all.

Pope, the Harvard psychiatrist with expertise in steroid use, said various studies have supported the notion of "'roid rage"—with users exhibiting irritability, aggressiveness, and sometimes violence, along with a disregard for the consequences.

Pope also cited problems associated with steroid withdrawal, particularly when a person abruptly stops using rather than cycles off the drugs by lowering the dosage in the final weeks. Among the symptoms are depression, disinterest, excessive sleeping, loss of appetite, and, in extreme cases, suicidal behavior.

A week after Garibaldi showed his mom the battered dresser, the Garibaldis received a call from USC's head baseball coach, Mike Gillespie. Rob had slept through practice.

Falling to Pieces

None of this made sense to Ray and Denise. Their once confident, outgoing, successful, and responsible kid was now falling apart. Garibaldi later told friends and family that he was getting teased a lot at USC both about his size and his learning disability. He told his family and friends that Gillespie called him stupid.

Garibaldi made his first admission to Cox about his use of steroids during a phone session the following May, when he said he was in the midst of a ten-week cycle of Deca.

Garibaldi also told Cox he had reduced his dosage of Effexor and intended to stop taking the drug altogether because he wanted to take steroids free of any interactions with other "mind-altering agents" that he was being prescribed, according to Cox's records.

Cox said he advised Garibaldi to stop using steroids, but Garibaldi said that he wanted to gain ten to fifteen pounds. He said he was getting the Deca from a source who was providing the same drug to several Oakland A's players. The A's declined comment.

"The irony is, he is telling me all this with the mind-set of a warrior," Cox said. "He was like a warrior going into battle, and he had to go through this sacrifice in order to sculpt his body into the perfect specimen."

Kicked Off the Team

Apparently nobody but Cox—who as Garibaldi's psychiatrist couldn't tell anyone—knew about the steroid use.

Things continued to deteriorate in the spring of 2001. There were repeated clashes with Gillespie, and Rob's behavior became increasingly erratic. His parents say they later were told by one of Rob's roommates that the other players who were living with him had begun locking their doors out of fear.

Finally, just weeks before USC was set to make another College World Series appearance in June 2001, Gillespie kicked Garibaldi off the team and took away his scholarship.

Garibaldi's allegations about his life at USC and treatment by his coach and teammates are not news to officials there.

"The best response from us would be that all these allegations that we've heard before, we've maintained are not true, and we have even maintained that we are prepared to file a defamation suit," said a USC spokesman.

The Final Act

Maytorena, Garibaldi's coach and friend since his Casa Grande days, said the young man told him about his steroid use sometime after returning from USC. Maytorena, now head baseball coach at Casa Grande, said he believed Rob was using both Deca and Sustanon at the same time, and he urged him to quit the drugs.

In the fall of 2001, Maytorena helped Garibaldi get lined up with his alma mater, Sonoma State, where he had played for coach John Goelz. Garibaldi seemed to start off relatively well, but his mental well-being quickly deteriorated—to the point that Goelz was having to write practice times on Garibaldi's wrist to make sure the outfielder wasn't late. Denise Garibaldi said she had to become her son's ultra-guardian.

"For the whole semester, I became his superego," she said. "I told him where he had to be at what time. I would write everything down for him. I put Post-Its in his car. I would talk to the teachers myself about what the assignments were."

How much or how often Garibaldi used steroids at Sonoma State is unclear. He would later tell his parents he took just one cycle during this time, beginning in the late spring of 2002. Maytorena said he believed Garibaldi did at least two cycles during his time at Sonoma State.

Unable to Quit

"He would back up cycles," Maytorena said. "You know, it got to the point where he would go back to back. . . . The way you gotta use that, you gotta cycle on and off, but he would do it and think that more was better. It got to the point where he thought, 'If I do another cycle, I can gain a little bit more and get a little stronger.'"

Garibaldi also apparently wasn't precise in his use, later telling his mother that he took "about this much" each time he injected, never mentioning an exact dosage.

The last few months of Garibaldi's life were tortured. There were admissions of steroid use, limited as they were. He told his mom first, on a Mother's Day camping trip, and pleaded with her not to tell his father.

She agreed, a decision that later would require her to do considerable repair work on her marriage. Denise said she decided to keep the information from her husband for several reasons: she was fearful how he would react; she believed Rob when he told her this would be his first and only time using and that he was doing it to prepare for the major league draft; she could talk to him freely and openly about the potential dangers of using the drugs; and he told her he would stop if she said his behavior became "too weird."

The major league draft was in June, and Rob saw it as his last chance.

Going Undrafted

Rob's brother Ray Jr. recalled Rob holed up in his room upstairs on draft day, while Denise remained downstairs panicked about what Rob would do if he wasn't picked.

"He comes out just with this blank look on his face and says, 'I didn't make it,'" Ray Jr. said. "He was totally depressed."

The secret between Rob and Denise ended about a month later when Goelz, the Sonoma State coach, called the Garibaldis to say he had heard Rob was using steroids. Now Ray Garibaldi knew, and he confronted Rob, asking what drugs he was on. Rob erupted and tried to choke his father.

Losing Control

There were further violent outbursts, and Rob even became delusional, prompting Denise to remind him of his promise to stop using steroids if he got too weird. By then, Rob was too far gone. He thought actress Cameron Diaz was going to come watch him play ball and then go on a date with him. He thought he was Jesus Christ. He talked to the television and thought it talked to him.

There were attempts to save Rob—such as a family intervention where he insisted, "I'm not a drug addict, I'm a ballplayer." The Garibaldis got him to try a rehab center. But shortly before his twenty-eight-day stint was scheduled to end, he was asked to leave after assaulting an employee.

Finally, four months after he confided to his mother, Rob stole a gun from a shooting range. About 3:30 the following morning, October 1, 2002, he started to leave the house and was stopped by his father. Rob said he was just going to get some food at Taco Bell and then take a drive—something he often did.

Three hours later, the Petaluma police were at the door, breaking the news that Rob had shot himself. He lived another eighteen hours before dying at a Santa Rosa hospital.

The Garibaldis had been keeping tabs on the mileage of Rob's car—they took away his use of the car for a time because of his unpredictable behavior—so they know he drove some two hundred miles that morning before returning to Petaluma and parking around the corner from the house.

Request for a Ballplayer

Ray Jr. likes to believe his baby brother toured all his old baseball haunts—from Little League fields in Foster City to the ballpark at Santa Rosa Junior College where he was better than anyone had ever been.

It was standing-room-only at the eight-hundred-seat church where Rob's funeral was held, befitting the kind of tribute paid to someone who made friends easily and who had once known how to light up a room.

Most of those people wouldn't have recognized the Rob who found himself in the car that October morning, with a gun in his left hand and all hope lost.

For Ray Garibaldi, the bitterness remains palpable, with much of his anger reserved for major league baseball and what he sees as public indifference to steroid use.

"I think it's sickening," the father said. "I think the public looks at baseball players as back in the gladiator days. They are just to entertain and if they want to screw themselves up, so what. But the problem is, no matter what anybody says, they are setting the bar for younger kids. And that bar is getting itself all the way down now to the junior high level."

He and Denise see hope, though, and this is what drives them to tell Rob's story.

Young Players Are in Danger

The Garibaldis have availed themselves not only to legislators trying to address the steroid and supplement problem, but have begun speaking to high school classes about Rob's life. Heather Campbell teaches a sports medicine class at Casa

Grande, and she brought in Ray and Denise last May to provide a human touch to her five-week segment on steroids and nutrition.

At one point, the Garibaldis asked the thirty-plus kids how many of them knew of high school students that have tried or are using steroids. More than twenty raised their hands. These are the people Ray and Denise Garibaldi desperately want to hear Rob's story.

"We are all better for having him in our lives," Denise said. "I think what happened was so tragic, so I want people to know that out of ignorance and trust, all this can happen."

The Excuses of Steroid Users

John Leo

*In this satirical essay, John Leo makes fun of athletes, their ste-
roid use, and their claims of innocence once they are caught red-
handed. He invites the high-paid professionals to take responsibility for their actions and come clean about drug use and steroid
abuse. John Leo has covered the social sciences and intellectual
trends for* Time *magazine and the* New York Times. *He is also
the author of two books:* Two Steps Ahead of the Thought Police *and a book of humor,* How the Russians Invented Baseball
and Other Essays of Enlightenment.

Rafael Palmeiro, the Baltimore Orioles star, told Congress
that he had absolutely, positively never used steroids, but
then he failed a urine test. So last week, he repeated his never-
ever statement but inserted a new word: He never intentionally used them. He said: "I am sure you will ask how I tested
positively for a banned substance. As I look back, I don't have
a specific answer to give. I wasn't able to explain how the
banned substance entered my body."

I can sympathize. A few years back, something quite similar happened to me. I got a ticket for speeding, and, being
personally above reproach, I quickly deduced that someone
had tinkered with my odometer and accelerator to create the
impression that I was somehow to blame for exceeding the
speed limit. Talk about unfair! Though understandably aggrieved, I paid the ticket. Later, I discovered that this happens
to people all the time. While you're sound asleep, some unknown person comes and tinkers with your car, or if you're an
athlete, with your personal bodily fluids. Understandably,
many of the athletes are bewildered when this occurs, protest-

John Leo, "Hey, It Wasn't My Fault," *U.S. News & World Report*, vol. 139, August 15,
2005, p. 28. Copyright 2005 *U.S. News & World Report*, L.P. All rights reserved. Re-
printed with permission.

ing innocence and shouting things like, "What? How many home runs did I hit last week? Why wasn't I told?"

It isn't just big stars like Barry Bonds and Palmeiro who are being victimized this way. It's also happening to obscure middle-relief pitchers with losing records. File it under "sports terrorism." Next, those skulking druggers will be gunning for innocent batboys, first-base coaches, and the guys who answer bullpen phones.

To their credit, some players who flunk their steroid test refuse to believe in secret nighttime visitors. Instead, after racking their brains for an answer, they conclude that somebody must have slipped them a contaminated Altoid. Or they announce that some apparently harmless diet supplement contained a steroid or an ingredient that mysteriously turned into a steroid in their body. "Evidently, I took a supplement of some sort that had a steroid derivative in it," Atlanta Falcons cornerback Ray Buchanan concluded a few years ago. Palmeiro's "never intentionally" explanation seemed to point the finger at supplements, though Associated Press reporter Alex Dominguez wrote that his "claims of ingesting steroids unintentionally were weakened by newspaper reports that the Orioles slugger tested positive for stanozolol, a powerful anabolic steroid not available in dietary supplements." Bonds explained that he took the now famous steroid products "the cream" and "the clear" in the belief that they were flaxseed oil and an arthritis rub. In 1999, Czech tennis player Petr Korda said he had no idea how the steroid nandrolene got into his system, though medical people told the news media that it could enter the body only through a large-bore needle. Some people probably believed that this finding tended to rule out the furtive nighttime drugging thesis, since a normally alert person like Korda might have noticed an intruder inserting an enormous needle into his body while he slumbered.

Lock up the Gatorade. Spiking the water or Gatorade of athletes is apparently another common way of inserting steroids into athletes without their consent. Canada's Ben Johnson offered this explanation when he failed his doping test after defeating U.S. athlete Carl Lewis in a famous race at the 1988 Olympics. Pole vaulter Janine Whitlock said something similar after testing positive for steroids at trials for the 2002 Commonwealth Games: "Of course I can't be 100 percent certain that anybody [spiked my drink], but I can't see any other way. You can't lock [drinks] away every time you take a vault, so it's possible." True enough. Locking up everyone's Gatorade bottle after each swig could sap the vitality of championship events.

One problem with the drink-spiking explanation, however, is that some victims, including Johnson, were found to have steroid levels associated with long-term use. Another difficulty is that athletes who ingest steroids by mistake often fail to notice that they then perform at amazing, if not superhuman, levels. At the 1988 Olympics, Johnson bolted out of the starting blocks with astounding force. Korda, though complaining of an ankle injury at Wimbledon, "went up for a smash," according to an opponent, "like he was Michael Jordan."

Ken Caminiti, the Houston Astros third baseman who died young from a drug overdose, estimated that at least half of the major-leaguers used steroids. Former major-league star Jose Canseco estimated it was 85 percent. But let's not get cynical. Most of the problem probably comes from those diet supplements, nighttime visitors, and all that spiked Gatorade.

CHAPTER 3

Perspectives on Steroid Use

Steroids, Double Standards, and Baseball

Jose Canseco

Jose Canseco was known for his slugging power and became the first player to hit forty home runs and steal forty bases in one season. In this selection he talks about playing with a young Mark McGwire in Oakland and injecting himself and his fellow player with steroids. Canseco also points out the discrepancy in treatment players of different ethnicities received. Whereas the Cuban player was quickly linked to and derided for his use of steroids, Mark McGwire—according to Canseco—got away with everything. Jose Canseco was Rookie of the Year in 1986 and won the American League MVP in 1988. He retired from base-ball in 2001.

McGwire in the Late 1980s

Mark McGwire showed as an Oakland A's rookie in 1987, my second full year in the major leagues, and I'll never forget what he looked like back then. I remember going down to Arizona for spring training that year and seeing this tall, skinny kid with basically no muscle on him whatsoever. He was six-five and weighed only 220 pounds.

But McGwire had one of the best—if not *the* best—right-handed power swings I'd ever seen in my life. I thought: "Wow, this guy has technique." He proved it was a great swing when he went out that season and hit forty-nine homers. He was named American League Rookie of the Year, so he and I were back-to-back Rookies of the Year.

Canseco and McGwire Use Steroids

Mark and I were a lot different, but from his first season with the A's, we became friendly. We were never really buddies, though. One of the main things we talked about was steroids—about how to tailor your doses and cycles to achieve the best results. We had access to the best steroids; it was like shopping from a high-end catalog.

Like me, Mark was curious about what different types of steroids could do for him, and how they could make him bigger and stronger. But he needed a little time to get used to the idea of actually using them, and so far as I know, he didn't actually start using steroids until after his rookie season. So the forty-nine home runs he hit that year probably came without any chemical enhancement.

The next year, 1988, Mark and I started talking about steroids again, and soon we started using them together. I injected Mark in the bathrooms at the Coliseum more times than I can remember. Sometimes we did it before batting practice, sometimes afterward. It was really no big deal. We would just slip away, get our syringes and vials, and head into the bathroom area of the clubhouse to inject each other.

Nobody knew that much about steroids back then and nobody really knew what we were doing. As the years went on, more and more players started talking to me about how they could get bigger, faster, stronger, but at that time, as far as I know, Mark and I were the only ones doing steroids.

The media dubbed us the Bash Brothers, but we were really the 'Roids Boys. Eventually, based on all that hype, I realized that people actually believed that we were living together, that we always hung out together, that we ate together, that we slept together. "Where's your other half?" people would ask. "Where's your brother?" It was laughable the way people built up these ideas in their minds based on a gimmicky slogan.

Personality Differences

We hung out here and there, but Mark didn't like to go out with me because the girls wouldn't pay any attention to him. They would all pay attention to me. That was mostly because of Mark. He was never the best-looking guy in the world. He felt awkward and out of place at clubs, plus he would never talk. I was quiet, too, but compared to Mark, I was a social dynamo. Mac just didn't like to go out because it felt like he was being overshadowed.

I always had a presence, and at the time, I was the most famous athlete in the world because of the way I looked, what I did to a baseball, and what I accomplished in the game. Also, I was a rebel and a rogue, and some people liked that edge. Mark was kind of a second-level star in those years, not nearly as famous as he would become later in the summer of 1998, but even so, he had things I did not. For starters, as a white all-American boy, he was accepted in a way I never could be as a Cuban. I guess at that time in the United States of America, it was taboo to have someone like me as an all-American hero.

There was this contrast between us, and from the very beginning, they pitted us against each other as competitors. Who's better? Who's stronger? Who hits the ball farther? Who is more dangerous? Mark always hated those comparisons, even more than I did.

I think it was only through using steroids and giving himself a new body that Mark really became more comfortable with himself, and stopped being quite so awkward around other people. I was the godfather of the steroid revolution in baseball, but McGwire was right there with me as a living, thriving example of what steroids could do to make you a better ball player.

Early in Mark's career, he went through the same transformation that I did. Suddenly, he was enormous. He developed these huge, muscular arms; his whole body was just massive. He kept with it and added more and more muscle mass. Later on, the year he and Sammy Sosa were both going after Roger Maris's single-season home-run record, McGwire would set the record, weighing in at 270 pounds.

Effects of Steroids

In recent years, as the public has come to understand how widespread steroid use has become in baseball, there's been a lot of speculation about where Mark's natural talent left off and the steroids kicked in. The answer is that steroids gave Mark strength and stamina—but they also gave him a more positive attitude.

The psychological effect of steroids is very dramatic. Using steroids properly can do wonders for your confidence. You look good. You're big and strong. McGwire was a twitching mass of muscle, and he had great technique. If that combination doesn't help you feel confident, I don't know what will.

The mind is a very powerful thing; if you convince yourself that you're a great player, and you have the basic ability, you're going to be a great player. You can have the perfect body for baseball and perfect ability, but if your brain is telling you "You have no chance!" you're not going to be successful. For Mark, steroids helped send his confidence level sky-high.

Being an All-American Hero

McGwire was a good twenty pounds heavier than I was, but guess what? For some reason, where McGwire was concerned, nobody ever mentioned steroids. What was going on? McGwire was already being groomed for superstardom. Baseball has always been on the lookout for players who could be packaged and marketed as all-American heroes, and McGwire was perfect for that: a big, awkward redhead with a natural home-run stroke. As all of us in baseball knew, McGwire was an untouchable. He was so protected by the powers that be in the game, it was incredible. No media outlet would even think of calling him into question, because there's no way they'd ever get an inside source.

To McGwire's credit, he was a little slow to understand what it was all about. I remember one time in the late 1980s, we were all sitting down together in the A's clubhouse talking about something that had appeared in one of the papers, declaring that Mark McGwire was the all-American boy and the all-American athlete. We mentioned it to McGwire, and I looked at him to see what he would say.

"Jose, I didn't want to be labeled like that," Mark told me.

I think he meant it, too.

"Mac, you know what?" I told him. "Now you're protected. You're protected by America. Nobody is going to touch you no matter what you do wrong."

It started to sink in with him that I was right.

"It's great to have that kind of backing by America," I told him. "You are set. You can never do anything wrong. You could rob a bank while raping a cheerleader and nothing would happen to you."

That's how the system works. There are some players who are protected by the system, and other players who the system abuses and takes advantage of, hanging them out to dry [exposing and abandoning them] and turning them into scapegoats [those who are falsely blamed]. It's disgusting the way baseball really works sometimes.

Walter Weiss, the shortstop who became the A's third straight Rookie of the Year in 1988, after me (1986) and McGwire (1987), once told me a story about the day when Mark and Walt were racing their cars after a game at the Coliseum, and this old lady was driving along really slow, and they forced her off the road. But what happened? Where was the media frenzy after that? Nowhere. After all, this was Mark McGwire, the golden boy, so everybody covered it up—the organization, the police, the media, everyone.

Media Prejudice Against Hispanics

Just imagine how an incident like that would have been handled if I had been involved. That was the pattern throughout our entire careers. Whether it was on a personal or professional level, you never heard the media breathe a bad word where it came to Mark McGwire. Everything was whitewashed. Meanwhile, my divorce was on national TV. That was how the deck was stacked, and Mark knew it and we all knew it: He could do no wrong, and I was always going to be the subject of controversy.

Think about if for a minute. How much of what people think they know about me goes back to the image of me portrayed in the media? How much of that feeds on itself, with people assuming they know what I'm like, and turning that into new controversies that convince more people that I'm all these bad things people say I am? Where does perception start and reality end? When does perception create reality?

The truth is, no one wants to face the fact that there was a huge double standard in baseball, and white athletes like Mark McGwire, Cal Ripken Jr., and Brady Anderson were protected and coddled in a way that an outspoken Latino like me never would be. The light-eyed and white-skinned were declared household names. Canseco the Cuban was left out in the cold, where racism and double standards rule.

Let's be honest: Back in 1988, no one wanted a Cuban to be the best baseball player in the world. Maybe it's different today, because there are so many great Latino superstars out there. But in 1987 and 1988, who were the great Latino ball players? There was only one; it was just me.

And when I became the first player ever to hit forty homers and forty stolen bases in one season, I was hands down the best player in the world. No one even came close. But who wanted a Cuban to be the best player in the world? Imagine doing something that had never been done in a major sport like baseball. I remember at the beginning of the 1988 season, the media guys asked me if I had any goals for the upcoming year.

"Well, I plan on doing the forty-forty—stealing forty bases and hitting forty home runs," I told them.

They laughed at me. I couldn't understand why.

"What's so hard about it?" I asked them.

"You know, no one's ever done it before," one of the reporters told me.

So what? I thought it was no big deal. "Well, I have the ability to do it," I said. "So why not do it?"

People always cite that example to prove I was ignorant. But who had the last laugh? I knew something the reporters didn't. I knew that all my hard work, and the right combination of steroids, had already made me a much better athlete than I had been before. I knew I was far beyond what any of them could conceive of in terms of my body and its capabilities.

Already by that point, I had become much faster, and even though I was up to 235 or 240 pounds, I had learned how to move that weight quickly. I incorporated technique with explosive speed, and I had enhanced my muscle-twitch fiber to be able to move much more quickly. Also, I knew that steroids would improve my stamina and keep me strong and explosive throughout the long baseball season. I incorporated all of that and did the forty-forty.

"That was great," my father finally said, but mostly he told other people that, not saying it to me directly.

The double standard began to kick in that year, at least when it came to media coverage. We won our division and went to Boston to play the Red Sox in the American League Championship Series, which we ended up sweeping. But suddenly you heard a lot of talk in the media: "Oh, Canseco had this forty-forty year because he's doing steroids—Oh, he's an obvious steroid user."

I remember one time Harmon Killebrew was doing commentary for a game between the A's and the Twins. When I came up to bat, he said: "I saw Canseco in the minor leagues and I've never seen a player change so much so drastically."

What a joke. How about McGwire? He went through an even more dramatic change than I did—you could see that just by comparing him in his rookie year with the A's, when everyone saw him, to how he looked a few years later. But nobody even cared what McGwire was doing.

He used to hide behind big, oversized shirts, but McGwire had the largest arms in baseball—twenty-one inches, and forearms like you wouldn't believe. But no one ever made an issue of it.

That was the pattern, from that year on. It started circulating a little bit that I might be doing steroids, and more and more reporters were criticizing me for gaining all this weight and stacking up the home runs. McGwire just kept getting bigger and bigger, but he was always protected by the media and by the organization.

And me? I was left out to dry.

I Lost My Son to Steroids

U.S. Drug Enforcement Administration

Taylor Hooton, a 17-year-old high school athlete from Plano, Texas, took his own life on July 15, 2003 as a result of the abuse of anabolic steroids. Only after his death did his parents become aware of the illegal use and abuse of anabolic steroids among high school athletes across the country. In this interview Hooton talks about the responsibility of professional athletes, and his work with the Drug Enforcement Administration. Don Hooton is the chairman and president of the Taylor Hooton Foundation for fighting steroid abuse based in Plano, Texas.

O*n losing his son and starting the Taylor Hooton Foundation.*

We were caught completely off guard when we lost Taylor. We had no idea of the high usage of steroids among our youth. We had no idea of the serious dangers of the drug and we had no experience with suicide itself. As we went through the healing process, and after talking to others, we found out we weren't the only ignorant people on this subject. We felt the need to reach out to our friends here in Plano (Texas) just to let them know how many of their kids were using this stuff. We met most of our friends at the ballpark, and we felt the need to reach out and tell them what happened, so hopefully it wouldn't happen to their kids. Little did we know that there was an information vacuum about steroids not only here in Plano, but nationally as well.

We are teaming up with Major League Baseball's Strength and Conditioning Coaches and the Drug Enforcement Administration to go into MLB stadiums beginning this summer [2007] to put on clinics—we call these clinics Hoot's Chalk

U.S. Drug Enforcement Administration, "Steroids and Our Youth: An Interview With Don Hooton," January 10, 2007. Reproduced by permission of the interviewee.

Talks. We will teach the local kids about the physical and psychological dangers of steroid abuse. Visualize—The kids will go to first base, where they will hear about the dangers of steroids as well as learn that to use them is to make a decision to cheat. Then, at second base the strength and conditioning coaches will teach these kids about how through proper diet and exercise it's possible to achieve their goals without using illegal steroids. Then at third base, they will have hitting and pitching coaches working with the kids on the fundamentals of baseball. Finally, DEA agents will talk to them in the stands and tell them that "if you haven't listened to anything so far, hear this—possession of anabolic steroids without a legitimate prescription is illegal and you can go to jail if you get caught with this stuff!"

We plan to be in six to eight stadiums this year and then hopefully all of the stadiums the following year. We will be starting in Cleveland this summer.

Working with the DEA . . .

I have had the opportunity to work with both sides of the DEA. I was unaware that there were two sides of the DEA. There is the law enforcement side which we see on TV and in the movies and there is also the demand reduction side—two very different but two very important pieces of the organization. I have had the opportunity to work with a lot of extremely competent people who want to reduce the demand for steroids. I also had the privilege to be aware of Operation Gear Grinder. It was an extremely impressive and professional operation. It resulted in the largest bust of steroids in U.S. history.

His thoughts on Barry Bonds and the controversy surrounding him . . .

Our focus is on the kids. What a 40-year-old man does with his own body is his own business, and to some extent I don't care. However, I do care about the impact that professional athletes' behavior has on the youth of our country.

These guys are role models—our kids look up to these guys and want to do anything they do to achieve their success. I'm tired of hearing that it wasn't against baseball rules to use steroids prior to 2002—it's been against federal law since the early 1990's.

On Jose Canseco, whose book Juiced *brought to light steroid abuse in and around Major League Baseball . . .*

You don't have to like the messenger to understand that the message he was delivering was accurate. I respect him for having the courage, regardless of his motivation, to step forward to shine the light on this. However, I disagree with him leaving the reader with the idea that steroids were a panacea to his success. That sends the absolute wrong message to kids.

On Mark McGwire speaking to the youth of America about the dangers of steroids . . .

I think it would send an extremely strong and positive message. During the congressional hearings, Mark McGwire said he would be a spokesperson against steroid abuse but in the year since, we have seen no evidence that he has stepped forward to speak to young people on this subject. We would welcome him to speak out on the issue. We would love to have him speak to kids on behalf of our foundation. I think it would be a very powerful message. He is still a very revered player and role model.

On whether or not Mark McGwire would be forgiven if he acknowledges having used steroids . . .

America is a forgiving society. It would be very difficult for me or anyone else to not forgive him if he admits he did something wrong. These guys are setting an example that as parents we have a very difficult time overcoming when we are sitting around the table trying to teach our children the lessons of life. Step up to the plate, admit what you were doing was wrong and take your punishment like a man—just like we would teach our 10- and 12-year-old kids to do if they got caught cheating at school.

Shouldn't we expect the same kind of behavior of those men and women who we have put up on a pedestal in society?

If Don Hooton was the commissioner of all professional sports . . .

The first thing we need to do is implement the World Anti-Doping Association code of what is considered a banned substance in sports. It's just not necessary for each and every league to develop and administer its own list of banned substances. There is a world standard and all sports should adopt this list.

We also need to adopt a meaningful and independent testing program that is truly random, and that is administered in such a way that leaves no doubt in anybody's mind that all athletes have a real opportunity to be tested multiple times throughout the year. This will mean that there is more than a reasonable chance that these guys and gals can be caught and not avoid the process because they are a star athlete.

And, we need to adopt the Olympic standard with respect to penalties. Regardless of the sport you are in, whether you are in high school, college or professional sports, the first time you get caught using banned performance enhancing drugs, you are banned from participating in sporting activities for two years. If you get caught a second time, you are out for life. Only then will we send a clear, strong and unquestionable message to the youth of the country that the use of performance enhancing drugs is just not acceptable.

On testifying before Congress and the future . . .

The hearings were important for a number of reasons. They raised awareness about steroid use among our youth. I'm pleased with Baseball Commissioner (Bud) Selig and the steps that have been taken to tighten up the penalties in professional baseball. However, steroid abuse is clearly not just a baseball problem. We make a big mistake when we focus solely on baseball. This problem cuts across all sports. Our objective is to make sure the spotlight remains just as hot on steroid use as it has been for the last year, and to widen it beyond the baseball field.

The battle is not over, but based on my experience working with the DEA, I have no doubt their team will make every effort possible to stop steroids from getting into our communities. We still have light years to go in order to tackle this problem with kids. We already have over a million kids who are using anabolic steroids. It's going to take all of us to make a difference.

What Steroids Did to Me

Dave Kindred

This text describes the effects of steroids from the point of view of a short-term user. In frank and informal language, the former weightlifter describes the thrill of trying to gain an edge and bulk up. After an initial high and feelings of power and strength, the young man started losing hair and fell into depression. Losing over fifty pounds in the aftermath of his drug experiment, he experienced severe health problems.

Dave Kindred has been a newspaper and magazine columnist for thirty-seven years, first in Mohammad Ali's hometown, Louisville, Kentucky. For many years, he covered sports for the Washington Post *and* Atlanta Journal-Constitution. *He is the 1991 winner of the Red Smith Award for lifetime achievement in sports journalism.*

Want to get scared? Read this. It's an e-mail from a young man in the Midwest. I had asked him to tell me about his experiences in our steroid age.

OK, here goes, informal, hope that's OK.

The E-mail Message

One of my buddies did steroids (juice) for a year on and off. Before he started, he was a good kid everyone loved to be around. After, he beat the crap out of his girlfriend daffy, beat up everyone else smaller than him and started in every illegal activity from theft to con scams.

I used to powerlift and bodybuild. About eighty-five percent of the males at my gym used steroids. A long list of professional athletes and bodybuilders frequented the gym and got their stuff. You could always find someone that had a bottle of testosterone or winstrol.

Half the guys, and a few girls, went completely nuts. Always getting into fights and trouble with the law, when before using the junk, they were good, honest kids. Yep, kids—about thirty percent of the roid users were under twenty. Why? Because the "big guys" are doing it, and there's nothing wrong with it, especially if the pros are doing it.

You Don't See the Negatives

One guy committed suicide after beating his live-in girlfriend. Me, I used steroids for four months, only four months. After I had already been a good powerlifter, natural my whole life. So why did I use, even after seeing the B.S. other guys went through? Because you don't see it when you are in that arena! You only see the positives, like being able to lift more weight than twenty people put together. The pump, the power that is experienced is greater and more addicting than anything I have encountered.

Many guys will do anything to feel that way, I mean anything! After using for only four months, my personality changed. I became depressed along with all of my buddies, I lost a lot of hair, my testes shrunk, my moods became uncontrollable. So I stopped completely. Well, it didn't end there. After a few months, my testosterone level was lower than a little girl's. My hormone levels were so messed up that I went even more nuts (no pun intended).

I couldn't sleep. My muscles were wasting. I went from a ripped 222 pounds to 170 in less than seven months. All of my joints hurt. I was sick all the time. I had no sex drive, even when confronted by the most beautiful girl. I continued to lose weight, my digestive system was totally off. I felt like crap. The doctors told me that I need to wait it out until I feel better. What? Until I feel better? When the hell will that be!?

No One Would Help

Soon I started having muscle twitches all over my body. How freaking annoying? I went from doctor to doctor, trying to find some help. No help? Even the doctor known for writing bogus prescriptions for roids wouldn't help me.

I looked in the mirror, and what did I see? Some little, weak, testosterone-less sicky. All for a few more pounds of muscle and strength! It's ironic, I started out pretty damn strong naturally, but using steroids I ended up weaker than when I started!

Even when I did steroids, I did my research on them—but not the right kind, the unbiased kind of research. It took me about four years to feel somewhat normal again. Four freaking years? For only four months of roiding!

Some of the short guys that I know that don't do roids anymore are still short, and now they're bald, weak and burned out. Many others have tumors growing somewhere or another in their bodies. Some have had heart, kidney, liver and lung problems. But some of them still use. Because if they stopped, they would feel one-hundred times worse than they do now.

Symptoms

If a steroid user doesn't come off a cycle properly, it creates so many problems. It would take me five pages to list them all. Most of them don't come off properly. Because they don't know how. Most of the pros and big-time athletes that were doing juice were monitored by a doctor at some point and had some clean roids to use. What do I mean by clean? A great deal of steroids came from Mexico, which didn't have any guidelines at all. And a lot of the stuff had worse stuff in it, especially the veterinarian stuff—yeah, juice made for animals.

Some guys would report having extreme flu-like symptoms after one shot of a Mexican steroid. Sometimes guys would break out in a purple rash that looked like really bad acne. (I bet half those guys have the hepatitis virus or something. Yuck!) And then they go ahead and share needles! Double yuck!

Some once-beautiful girls now look like ugly men? Some guys get "roid butt"—after an injection, the juice doesn't absorb properly, and a big cyst develops. It hurts and looks horrible.

The stuff used by pro and Olympic athletes is better than the average guy's, way complex and way expensive, especially with doctors to monitor them. And there are many ways to fool a test. So why worry, except it's your life you're ruining.

Here, I have only one thing to add.

Heaven help us.

CONTEMPORARY
ISSUES
COMPANION

CHAPTER 4

How Should Society Deal with Steroid Use?

If They Work,
Why Ban Them?

Jose Canseco

*Instead of being banned, Jose Canseco argues in this article, ste-
roids should be allowed and their use should be monitored by
knowledgeable personnel. Taking himself as a positive example,
Canseco explains the many mental and physical benefits steroids
can have for the athlete. In his opinion a steroid ban won't stop
athletes from using drugs, but it will perpetuate misinformation
and malpractice and put users in serious danger. Jose Canseco
was Rookie of the Year in 1986 and won the American League
MVP (Most Valuable Player) in 1988. He retired from baseball
in 2001.*

Steroids Are the New Drug

People insist on thinking of steroid use in negative terms, as
though it's a sickness, when in fact most people who use steroids properly end up a lot more healthy than when they
started. Here is something to think about: When I first came
into the league, major league baseball players partied a whole
lot more than they do now. Back then, in the late 1980s, a lot
of guys were doing recreational drugs, and of course drinking
a lot. That has changed drastically.

As the years went by, and the players got more into steroids, weight lifting, and good nutrition, for most players the
other drugs went by the wayside—liquor, cocaine, marijuana.
When the guys realized that steroids worked, that was all they
cared about. They looked better, they were stronger, they could
perform at a higher level and land that big contract everyone
wanted. So if there were certain sacrifices to make—like cut-

ting back on drinking—that was no big deal. It was just one of those things that happened naturally. There are still exceptions, like that amazing partier Jason Giambi, but for most baseball players, the steroid era meant a new focus on clean living.

Health Considerations

There are health considerations, obviously. You don't want to put too much stress on your liver with your steroid regimen. You have to look out for dangerous combinations, because your liver can't handle being stressed in three different ways at once. If you are overusing steroids, and you're also using cocaine and liquor, you've got a big problem.

So what does the smart athlete do? He uses no cocaine, no marijuana, no ecstasy, no liquor, and only a moderate amount of steroids, administered properly—and, ka-ching, he's on his way to those million-dollar contracts. That's a smart player. He lets the liver work at its normal pace, filtering out the steroid residue, and he ends up healthy, wealthy, and wise.

Amphetamines

The one other drug that's still hanging on in baseball is amphetamines, which have always been a big part of the game. Call them what you want—pep pills, greenies, dextroamphetamine sulfate—they've been around a long time. In Jim Bouton's famous 1980 book *Ball Four*, he was the first one to talk about greenies in public. He quoted the player named Tommy Davis, saying, "How fabulous are greenies? The answer is very," Bouton continued. "A lot of baseball players couldn't function without them."

Elsewhere in the book, Bouton describes a player who had recently received a supply of 500 greenies. "That ought to last about a month," Bouton wrote.

Greenies were everywhere when I first came into the league. I would say that at least eight out of ten players were taking greenies back then; they may have been as widespread as steroids are now. They were as acceptable as popping aspirin. Some guys would mix greenies with Excedrin or another caffeine-laced product. That's old school. It goes all the way back to the early days of baseball. Especially when they had a day game after a night game, players would need a little boost waking up. They'd take a pep pill an hour or so before the game, and by first pitch they'd have some extra spring in their step.

Greenies are still around, but now the guys who take them are the exceptions. Why the big change? Again, the number one reason is steroids. I never took a greenie. I just didn't see any point. Steroids get you going. They accelerate your heart rate to the point where you don't need a stimulant to pick you up. A few players may have used a combination of both, but that's really just a few guys who like to be incredibly wired. When steroids became widespread in baseball, I think most everybody realized that mixing them with amphetamines can have an adverse reaction on you. That's when you saw greenies start to disappear from clubhouses.

The decline in amphetamines was part of the general trend toward better fitness that came with steroid use. With salaries getting so high—and even utility players bringing in $3 million a year—the smart players realized that the better care they took of themselves, the more they kept their bodies strong with steroids and good nutrition, the more years they'd be able to play—and the more money they'd make. For a while everybody was on the fitness kick, eating right, taking steroids, getting the right amount of sleep. So you saw bigger, stronger, faster, and *healthier* athletes, instead of those raggedy, run-down, pot-bellied ball players of previous eras.

If you were to take a few contemporary major-league teams, and strip down all the players, you would find that most ballplayers have pretty good bodies. They're strong and fit, compared to thirty or forty years ago. It'll be interesting to see how that changes if more players start backing off of steroids. Even though major-league baseball hasn't done anything serious to discourage players from using steroids, there's still a lot of concern about what's going to happen in the next couple years. So there's been a movement of guys changing how they use steroids—some of them using less, some quitting altogether.

For those guys who decide not to use steroids any more, it's still possible to maintain about 80 percent of the muscle mass they have gained, if they go about it the right way. And the smart ones will consider using a low dose of steroids all year round.

Avoiding Getting Caught

Some of the players, I'm sure, are thinking of quitting just because they're afraid of being caught. But that's always been a fear, and we were always careful. One obvious precaution most of us did take was doing the majority of our injections at home—that is, not taking them on the road with us. On an especially long road trip, we might make an exception, but in general the trips were eight or ten days, so the players knew they'd be fine if they injected right before the trip started and again right after we got back.

But the average baseball player shouldn't really be ashamed of his steroid use. Because the people who really abuse steroids aren't baseball players at all. It's the bodybuilders, football players, and contenders in world's-strongest-men competitions who have pushed things too far and given steroids a bad name. They're the ones who apparently believe that more is always better—when actually more is usually too much.

Carefully controlling the amounts of steroids you take, administering them at the proper time—that's the way to make them work for you, without risking your health. Like most chemicals that can help you, steroids would be dangerous if used in too large a quantity. Just consider the example of

Botox, whose popularity has now spread from Hollywood. As most people know, Botox is used to paralyze muscles to stop the aging process in the face. But Botox is also poisonous—it's a form of botulism, the poison, which can kill you. The key is knowing how to use it without taking undue risks. That's exactly the way to think of steroids: Sure, they can be deadly if used in ridiculously large amounts, the way some out-of-control weight-lifters do. But if you're smart, and careful, and know what you're doing, you can use them to reach your true potential.

The Future of Steroids

Charles E. Yesalis and Virginia S. Cowart

Charles Yesalis and Virginia Cowart take a look at the future of performance enhancing drugs in sports and conclude that if we want to change athletes' lives, we first have to change how our society views athletic performances. If winning is everything, and if we are taught that only winning counts, we only encourage teen, college, and professional athletes to bend or break the rules and search for new drugs that won't be detected by doping tests. Charles Yesalis directed the first national study of steroid use among adolescents. He is a professor of health policy and administration and exercise and sport science at Pennsylvania State University. Virginia Cowart has been a contributor to many sports medicine publications.

Looking to the future, it is easy to identify the hazards that performance-enhancing drugs bring to sports, but it is hard to agree on an appropriate course of action and follow it. In addition to steroid abuse, athletes also are using human growth hormone, insulin-like growth factor, erythropoietin, and a myriad of other drugs. As researchers continue to unlock the chemical secrets of the human body, it is reasonable to assume that additional drugs that confer an athletic advantage will be developed. If Americans cannot agree on how to deal with the drugs we have now, there can be no basis for deciding how to handle future drugs that may be used to alter physiology or psychology.

This problem is not new. Cheating was known even in the original Olympic games in ancient Greece. In the modern world, man's capacity to alter body and mind brings a new dimension to an old problem. At the 1993 Prague Conference on Steroids, delegates agreed on a series of reasons why performance enhancement in sports is unacceptable, including the following:

- An athlete may suffer physical or psychological harm because of his drug use.

- Drug use contaminates sports because the results are obtained by unnatural means. An athlete who uses drugs has an unfair advantage over one who does not.

- The use of anabolic steroids is cheating and violates the rules of virtually every sport.

- The use of steroids for nonmedical purposes is a violation of state and federal laws.

- The use of drugs by one athlete may coerce or force another to use them to maintain equality.

- High school students and younger individuals are using these drugs.

If the only thing wrong with steroids were a risk to health, an athlete would be justified in taking a position that it is a matter of individual choice whether to accept that risk. However, these drugs have the power to fundamentally change the contest because they change the strength and power of the contestants. Therefore, the ethical and moral must be addressed.

A Focus on Winning

The fact is that the appetite for steroids and other performance-enhancing drugs has been created predominantly by a societal fixation on winning and physical appearance. This behavior is learned. Children play games for fun, at least as long as they can before adults intervene to tell them that winning is what's important. One of the strongest reasons we should not give up the struggle to make sports contests fair and to encourage young athletes to be good sportsmen is because their ethical conduct on the playing field lays a foundation for later ethical conduct in life. Life is a team sport. Competitiveness and a fierce desire to win are qualities that have made this nation great. But before we allow our children to compete, we must first establish in them a moral and ethical foundation so they have boundaries they will not cross in pursuit of victory.

Overcoming Stereotypes

"Show me a good and gracious loser and I'll show you a failure," said Notre Dame's legendary football coach Knute Rockne, but children need to learn how to do their best, how to win, and how to lose. Sadly, youngsters who participate in sports, particularly those with athletic ability, often find themselves enmeshed in highly stressful situations early in life when they should still be learning what it takes to be a decent person. There are examples in every sport of young athletes who drop out because they were pushed too fast. They end up with psychic burnout or develop overuse injuries at a young age. Other young athletes may be tempted to resort to drugs. When children are inculcated with a "winning is the *only* thing" attitude, performance-enhancing drug use and other forms of cheating become very rational behavior.

When youth sports stops being about skills development and being part of a team effort and starts being consumed with winning, kids learn another lesson. They become afraid of losing, and too many of them grow up afraid to take chances because they might not be successful. The incomparable Michael Jordan has said he doesn't fear losing; it is "not trying" that he can't accept. If kids grow up wanting to "be like Mike," let us hope they try to emulate his attitude as much as his basketball skills.

Societal Attitudes and National Pride

If we decide that the use of performance-enhancing drugs may cause fundamental changes in the nature of sports that are not acceptable, the question then becomes: Can we change societal attitudes? Health educators have made some inroads in changing several high-risk behaviors, such as high-fat diets, sedentary lifestyles, and smoking. They have been able to do this, in part, because a wealth of scientific data exists that correlates habits and health risks. Some individuals have made lifestyle changes because the attitudes of society toward health risks have changed, and now there is public disapproval of some risky behaviors. Drunk driving and smoking have been altered by changed attitudes in society.

Turning to sports, the first obvious difference is that anabolic steroids don't usually cause athletes to behave in ways that bring public disapproval. They often demonstrate improvements in physical performance and appearance. Society is much less likely to shun these people. In fact, the adulation of fans, the media, and peers serves as a strong reinforcement, as do the financial, material, and sexual rewards that come with athletic success.

Is Winning Everything?

When it comes to international sports, there is an added element of national pride. For several years before the 1996 Olympic Games, there was great concern about the Chinese female athletes who would be coming to Atlanta. Press coverage had focused attention on the exploits of the Chinese women and stimulated public concern about whether a fair contest would be possible. A 1995 *Sports Illustrated* article noted that Chinese distance runners were doing an incredible volume of training. Women ran almost a marathon a day at higher altitudes, and then followed that up with sprint training. This type of training schedule flies in the face of stress studies that have demonstrated that humans don't have enough adaptive energy to do both.

The story in swimming was much the same. FINA, the international sports governing body for swimming, keeps track of the top twenty-five times recorded each year for each of the recognized events in swimming. When FINA issued the 1992 top twenty-five rankings, only twenty-eight Chinese women made the list of 325. In 1993, the Chinese women had 101 top twenty-five rankings out of a total of 325. This is an enormous change over a very short period of time. The fact that China has only eight male swimmers who achieved top twenty-five rankings raises the index of suspicion about drug use even more because women make proportionally greater gains on steroids. It began to sound far too much like the East German story where the female swimmers came from nowhere in the 1970s and then dominated women's swimming for a decade. After the Berlin Wall fell, the world learned that sophisticated treatment with steroids and other drugs was the foundation of the East German success.

National Interests Dictate Sports

The Chinese women did not dominate in Atlanta, however. Drug testing at the Asian Games preceding the 1996 Olympics caught some Chinese female athletes who were using steroids. Some of these women have since dropped from public view in their sports. It is unlikely the story of why the Chinese female athletes receded from their dominant position before the Games will ever be known, but public opinion may have played a part. Communist China, at least in the recent past, obviously intends to use international athletics as a means to showcase its society. Because China is a closed society, and the State controls the pharmaceutical industry, they have the motive and opportunity to develop designer drugs and perfect other strategies to subvert drug testing.

Alternatives for Action

What are the alternatives for dealing with steroids and other performance-enhancing drugs? They include legalization, legislation and enforcement, education, and/or changing societal values and attitudes about physical appearance and winning in sports. The first, legalizing drugs, would force virtually all athletes to become drug users if they wanted to be competitive, and it would reinforce the notion that any action in the service of winning is OK. That alternative is clearly unacceptable. Some people contend, however, that athletes in certain sports are already faced with the dilemma of using drugs or accepting that they cannot be truly competitive.

Denial Is Not a Way Out

An alternative solution is to deny that a serious problem exists. Many sports fans are currently embracing this alternative because it does not conflict with a fixation on winning and appearance. The formula for this alternative is fairly simple. First, turn a blind eye to obvious signs of drug use like athletes of superhuman size, strength, or speed. Next, publicly proclaim victory over the problem because drug testing exists, even though it has many obvious loopholes. Finally, hang an anti-steroid poster in the school weight room and schedule the annual showing of a video depicting the evils of steroids.

It takes courage to abandon this highly seductive strategy of denial, but if we do, real progress is possible. At the close of the Steroid Congress in Prague, twelve recommendations were issued that offer some hope for developing alternative strategies for dealing with steroids if they can be implemented:

- Further research on public health and social consequences should be encouraged.

- Governments and international organizations should share information.

- National and international laboratories should consider collecting and sharing reference standards and analytical methodologies.

- Health, police, customs, and policy officials involved in the issues of drug control, abuse, and trafficking should familiarize themselves with the available information on steroids.

- Prevention efforts should be strengthened.

- Both governments and sports bodies should enhance their progress in detecting the use of anabolic steroids.

- Legislation should be looked at with a view to strengthening controls over anabolic steroids.

- National regulatory authorities and sports organizations should cooperate in developing a joint strategy to combat the abuse of anabolic steroids.

- National authorities should consider increasing cooperation on international commerce of anabolic agents.

- Police and customs authorities should provide operational assistance to each other in the investigation of trafficking in anabolic steroids.

- The ICPO/Interpol [International Criminal Police Organization] and Customs Cooperation Council should continue to collect, review, and analyze existing information so as to assist in developing programs on anabolic steroid abuse and trafficking.

- The World Health Organization should continue its analysis of global trends regarding the use and abuse of anabolic agents and its assessment of current educational, prevention, and regulatory activities.

Will any of these recommendations, if implemented, change the level of drug use at the professional and Olympic levels? Probably not. There is simply too much money at stake, and many of the drugs work too well to think otherwise. The health and spiritual well-being of our children are so vital that we can ill afford to throw up our hands in despair.

Beyond education, we are left with the struggle to change the values of society. Whether it is possible to change an unhealthy preoccupation with winning at any cost remains to be seen. Far too many of us focus on the individual rewards of athletic success but fail to realize that professional sports careers are only a dream for all but a very few people. For example, even with thirty teams in the National Football League, there is room for less than 1,500 players. The probability of a high school athlete collecting a paycheck in the NBA or NFL is about 1/10,000.

Myths Don't Help Children

In tennis, there are hundreds of professionals, but only a few receive appearance fees and tournament winnings. The same is true in golf and other professional sports. Only a handful of Olympic athletes are ever able to capitalize on their sports success. Clearly, preparing for a career in professional sports is risky business because it requires focusing on getting a job that, statistically, doesn't exist. The available data indicate that misguided parents and coaches help perpetuate the idea of the "Rocky" story when the reality is that they have almost as good a chance to win the lottery as to guide a child into professional sports. Moreover, this attitude sends an unspoken message that participating in sports is not worth anything unless the participant can parlay that into a paying job.

There are those who argue that our attitudes and values related to sports and appearance are too deeply entrenched to change, and that may be true. If it is, we must resign ourselves to the prospect of children and teens using dangerous drugs with known short-term and unknown long-term negative health consequences. It certainly is true that no amount of legislation or drug testing will work unless society does decide that its fixation with winning and appearance is unhealthy. But the individual and societal rewards of changing our attitudes and making sports competition a healthy activity make the goal worth the pursuit.

States Legislate on Steroid Use

Mark Sappenfield

In this article, author Mark Sappenfield discusses the growing trend of steroid use in teenagers and how states are taking action to reduce steroid use in high schools. He writes about how states are trying to enforce steroid testing on student athletes, but that these tests raise concerns regarding both privacy and cost. Sappenfield explains how some states have set more modest goals in hopes of decreasing steroid use. Mark Sappenfield is a staff writer for the Christian Science Monitor.

A surge of activity in high schools and state legislatures from Connecticut to California suggests that the outrage over steroid abuse has now made it to Main Street America.

For years, illegal steroid use had been seen almost exclusively as the scourge of high-stakes sports—the far-off realm of millionaire ballplayers and athletes of freakish physical proportions. But the March congressional hearing, which included not only an evasive Mark McGwire [a professional baseball player] but also the parents of a high-schooler whose suicide was linked to steroids, has provided momentum to schools and lawmakers seeking to root out teen use of performance-enhancing drugs.

States Plan Steroid Rules For High-Schoolers

In May 2005, California became the first state to establish steroid rules specifically for high-schoolers, including a requirement that all its athletes and their parents sign an antisteroid contract. Seven states are also considering bills that range from tougher penalties for steroid dealers to broad testing of teen athletes.

Mark Sappenfield, "States Taking on Teen Steroid Use," *The Christian Science Monitor*, Boston, MA: May 9, 2005. Copyright © 2005 The Christian Science Publishing Society. All rights reserved. Reproduced by permission from Christian Science Monitor, (www.csmonitor.com).

Most plans are limited in scope for now, focusing on education more than enforcement. The cost of steroid testing is prohibitive, many states and school districts say, and the legal questions are troublesome. But the flurry of bills represents an awakening, as Americans come to realize that the synthetic absurdity of the East German Olympic teams of the 1970s and 1980s has spread much closer to home.

"Right now, because of the hearings in Washington, it is a topic of high interest nationwide," says Jerry Diehl of the National Federation of State High School Associations in Indianapolis. "Local communities are wanting to keep these performance-enhancing substances out of the hands of adolescents."

Steroid Use Is A Growing Trend

Between 1991 and 2003, the number of high schoolers who said they took steroids at least once more than doubled to 6 percent, according to the Centers for Disease Control and Prevention. Steroid use cuts across gender lines as well. A recent government-sponsored study of risky behaviors found that 5 percent of high school girls and 7 percent of middle-school girls admit to trying anabolic steroids at least once.

The numbers, while not overwhelming, point to a trend that is generating concern nationwide.

A week before the congressional steroid hearings, with its testimony of high-school steroid abuse, five students in Connecticut were arrested for possessing and passing out steroids they bought on vacation in Mexico. The school was the state's football champion.

Since then, three states have taken steps to initiate comprehensive steroid testing among high schoolers. In April 2005, the Florida House unanimously passed a bill to establish a pilot program, which would test athletes in one sport statewide. Meanwhile, a Connecticut lawmaker and the New

Mexico governor have proposed setting aside state money to create random testing for all high-school athletes.

Testing Raises Privacy Concerns

These efforts have quickly become the focus of the national debate. While virtually everyone agrees about the dangers of steroids and the desire to eliminate them from high-school locker rooms, the question of testing causes deep divisions.

On one hand, testing is considered the most effective deterrent. On the other, the process—though consistently supported by the courts—raises privacy concerns. Moreover, it casts schools in the role of an anti-doping agency and potentially the target of angry parents.

"It's inevitable that you will get a parent who will challenge the drug test" in court, says Frank Uryasz, president of the National Center for Drug-Free Sport in Kansas City, Mo. "Any high school district should build into its budget the cost of defending its drug-testing program—and that might not be a small cost."

States Set More Modest Goals

In states with tight budgets, even the cost of steroid tests—as much as $150 each—can be a nonstarter. As a result, many have set more modest goals:

- One Texas state representative, who wanted to mandate testing for all athletes on high-school playoff teams, is now pushing a bill that would establish education programs for students, parents, and coaches.

- In Michigan, the House recently passed a bill that would require high schools to ban students from sports if they abused steroids—though there was no provision for testing.

- Minnesota has taken a different tack altogether, with a bill to increase penalties for selling steroids illegally, including extra jail time if dealers sell to minors.

In May 2005, the California Interscholastic Federation, which administers high-school sports in the state, took a similar go-slow approach. It approved new rules, which include a requirement for every coach to complete steroid education this year, and for every school to come up with an anti-steroid policy to be signed by its athletes and their parents.

Budgets Pose Problems

Testing would be "helpful," says spokeswoman Emmy Zack. "But now, it's just not possible because of the financial situation."

Connecticut's proposed pilot program, for example, would cost $200,000—enough for 2,000 tests, covering less than 2 percent of the state's 95,000 high-school athletes.

In California, though, the fact that the state has some 700,000 high-school athletes and a multibillion-dollar budget deficit means that testing is, for now, off the table.

"Nobody wants kids doing [steroids], but how is [the testing] going to get paid for?" asks Rick Francis, president of the California State Athletic Directors Association. "Most districts are not going to do it when they can't even pay for textbooks."

Organizations to Contact

The editors have compiled the following list of organizations concerned with the issues presented in this book. The descriptions are derived from materials provided by the organizations. All have publications or information available for interested readers. The list was compiled on the date of publication of the present volume; the information provided here may change. Be aware that many organizations take several weeks or longer to respond to inquiries, so allow as much time as possible.

American Academy of Pediatrics (AAP)
American Academy of Pediatrics
Elk Grove Village, IL   60007-1098
(847) 434-4000 • fax: (847) 434-8000
Web site: www.aap.org

The American Academy of Pediatrics (AAP) and its member pediatricians dedicate their efforts and resources to the health, safety, and well-being of infants, children, adolescents, and young adults. The AAP has approximately sixty thousand members in the United States, Canada, and Latin America. The mission of the American Academy of Pediatrics is to attain optimal physical, mental and social health, and well-being for all infants, children, adolescents, and young adults. The organization publishes the periodicals *Pediatrics* and *AAP News*, as well as books on children's health.

American College of Sports Medicine (ACSM)
PO Box 1440, Indianapolis, IN   46206
(317) 637-9200 • fax: (317) 634-7817
Web site: www.acsm.org

The largest sports medicine and exercise science organization in the world, ACSM has more than twenty thousand international, national, and regional chapter members. This organization is a good source of information on the risks of performance-enhancing drugs such as steroids and human growth hormone. The ACSM publishes the journals *Medicine & Science in Sports & Exercise, Exercise and Sport Sciences Reviews*, and ACSM's *Health & Fitness Journal*.

Athletes Against Steroids (AAS)
e-mail: tomc@athletesagainststeroids.org
Web site: www.athletesagainststeroids.org

The mission of Athletes Against Steroids (AAS) is to educate amateur and professional athletes, students, coaches, personal trainers, sports researchers, nutritional companies, educators, magazine publishers, and other groups on the dangers of steroids. The AAS Web site provides readers with links to pertinent news and articles and publishes its own e-newsletter.

Center for the Study of Sport in Society
Northeastern University, Boston, MA   02115
(617) 373-4025 • fax: (617) 373-4566
Web site: www.sportinsociety.org

The Center's mission is to increase awareness of sport and its relation to society and to develop programs that identify problems, offer solutions, and promote the benefits of sport. Programs include National Student Athlete Day and the Degree Completion Program. Center publications include the annual *Racial Report Card* and an annual report.

National Alliance for Youth Sports
2050 Vista Pkwy., West Palm Beach, FL   33411
(561) 684-1141 • fax: (561) 684-2546
e-mail: nays@nays.org
Web site: www.nays.org

The National Alliance for Youth Sports is a nonprofit organization that works to provide safe, enjoyable, and positive sports for youth in the United States. It provides certification programs for coaches, officials, and administrators and participates in programs to prevent child abuse and encourage parental involvement in youth sports. The alliance operates a National Clearinghouse for Youth Sports Information that provides access to many publications and instructional materials pertaining to youth sports.

National Collegiate Athletic Association (NCAA)
6201 College Blvd., Overland Park, KS 66211-2422
(913) 339-1906
Web site: http://ncaa.org

The NCAA is the national administrative body overseeing all intercollegiate athletics. It publishes up-to-date information on regulations (including those concerning drugs) for college athletes in the United States, as well as health and safety brochures.

National High School Athletic Coaches Association (NHSACA)
PO Box 5020, Winter Park, FL 32793
(407) 679-1414
e-mail: office@hscoaches.org
Web site: www.hscoaches.org

The NHSACA seeks to promote cooperation among coaches, school administrators, the press, and the public. It holds seminars in sports medicine and promotes educational programs on drug abuse awareness.

National Institute on Drug Abuse (NIDA)
6001 Executive Blvd., Bethesda, MD 20892-9561
(301) 443-1124
e-mail: information@nida.nih.gov
Web site: www.nida.nih.gov

In addition to general drug abuse prevention programs and other research efforts, NIDA also invests in public education efforts to increase awareness about the dangers of steroid abuse. NIDA publishes brochures and books on drug use for teenagers.

U.S. Olympic Committee (USOC)
1750 East Boulder St., Colorado Springs, CO   80909
(719) 632-5551
Web site: http://usoc.org

Like other national Olympic committees around the world, the USOC publishes codes of ethics to which Olympic athletes are expected to adhere. The USOC also has compiled a detailed list of drugs athletes are banned from using in competition.

Bibliography

Books

David Aretha — *Steroids and Other Performance-enhancing Drugs.* Berkeley Heights, NJ: MyReportLinks.com Books, 2005.

Dynise Balcavage — *Steroids.* Philadelphia: Chelsea House Publishers, 2000.

John C. Bartone — *Sports—and What's New with Anabolic Steroids, Including Uses, Risks, and Dangers.* Washington, DC: AABE Publishers Association, 2001.

John C. Bartone and Hugo H. Bronsen — *Sports and Anabolic Steroids: Index of Modern Information.* Washington, DC: AABE Publishers Association, 2001.

Christopher N. Burns — *Doping in Sports.* New York: Nova Science Publishers, 2006.

Center for Substance Abuse Treatment (U.S.) — *Anabolic Steroids.* Columbia, MD: U.S. Department of Health and Human Services, 2006.

Steven B. Karch — *Karch's Pathology of Drug Abuse.* Boca Raton, FL: CRC Press, 2002.

Cynthia Kuhn, Scott Swartzwelder, Wilkie Wilson, et al. — *Buzzed: The Straight Facts About the Most Used and Abused Drugs from Alcohol to Ecstasy.* New York: W.W. Norton, 1998.

Pat Lenahan — *Anabolic Steroids: And Other Performance-enhancing Drugs.* New York: Taylor & Francis, 2003.

Suzanne LeVert — *The Facts About Steroids.* Tarrytown, NY: Benchmark Books, 2005.

Richard Mintzer — *Steroids=Busted!* Berkeley Heights, NJ: Enslow Publishers, 2006.

Lee F. Monaghan — *Bodybuilding, Drugs and Risk.* New York: Routledge, 2001.

Judy Monroe — *Steroids, Sports, and Body Image: The Risks of Performance-enhancing Drugs.* Berkeley Heights, NJ: Enslow Publishers, 2004.

National Institute on Drug Abuse — *Anabolic Steroids.* Bethesda, MD: National Institute on Drug Abuse, U.S. Department of Health and Human Services, National Institutes of Health, 2002.

James N. Parker and Philip M. Parker — *Anabolic Steroids: A Medical Dictionary, Bibliography, and Annotated Guide to Internet References.* San Diego, CA: Icon Group International, 2003.

James N. Parker and Philip M. Parker — *The Official Patient's Sourcebook on Anabolic Steroid Dependence.* San Diego, CA: Icon Health Publications, 2002.

Lisa Rogak — *Steroids: Dangerous Game.* Minneapolis, MN: Lerner Publications, 1992.

Albert Spring   *Steroids and Your Muscles: The Incredibly Disgusting Story.* New York: Rosen Central, 2001.

William N. Taylor   *Anabolic Steroids and the Athlete.* Jefferson, NC: McFarland, 2002.

Steven Ungerleider   *Faust's Gold: Inside the East German Doping Machine.* New York: Thomas Dunne Books/St. Martin's Press, 2001.

James Edward Wright and Virginia S. Cowart   *Anabolic Steroids: Altered States.* Carmel, IN: Benchmark Press, 1990.

Charles E. Yesalis, ed.   *Anabolic Steroids in Sport and Exercise.* Champaign, IL: Human Kinetics, 2000.

Periodicals

Howard Bryant   "A Tainted Era? Boom Years for the National Pastime, but Drug Issue Takes a Deep Cut at Game's Image," *Boston Herald Sports*, February 2004.

Howard Bryant   "A Tainted Era? Creatine, Growth Hormones, Steroids," *Boston Herald Sports*, February 2004.

Howard Bryant   "A Tainted Era? Guilty or Not, Players Are Feeling Fans' Skepticism as Offensive Numbers Escalate," *Boston Herald Sports*, March 2004.

P.M. Clarks and H.S. Thompson — "Drugs and Sport: Research Findings and Limitations," *Sports Medicine*, December 1997.

Larry Cohen, Craig Hartford, and Geoff Rogers — "Lipoprotein (a) and Cholesterol in Body Builders Using Anabolic Androgenic Steroids," *Medicine & Science in Sports & Exercise*, February 1996.

Sara F. Farrell and Marilyn Y. McGinnis — "Long-term Effects of Pubertal Anabolic-androgenic Steroid Exposure on Reproductive and Aggressive Behaviors in Male Rats," *Hormones and Behavior*, 2004.

Stephen Fraser — "Destroyed by 'Roids," *Current Health*, January 2005.

Gary Green, Don Catlin, and Borislav Starcevic — "Analysis of Over-the-Counter Dietary Supplements," *Clinical Journal of Sport Medicine*, October 2001.

Gary Green, Don Catlin, Borislav Starcevic, Frank Uryasz, Todd Petr, and Corey Bray — "NCAA Study of Substance Use and Abuse Habits of College Student-Athletes," *Clinical Journal of Sport Medicine*, January 2001.

Herbert A. Haupt — "Anabolic Steroids and Growth Hormone," *American Journal of Sports Medicine*, June 1993.

Peter Hoaken and Sherry Stewart — "Drugs of Abuse and the Elicitation of Human Aggressive Behavior," *Addictive Behaviors*, 2003.

Fawzi Kadi, Anders Eriksson, Staffan Holmner, Lars-Eric Thornell — "Effects of Anabolic Steroids on the Muscle Cells of Strength-trained Athletes," *Medicine & Science in Sports & Exercise*, November 1999.

M.I. Kalinski, C.C. Dunbar, and Z. Szygula — "Research on Anabolic Steroids in the Former Soviet Union," *Medicine & Science in Sports & Exercise*, May 2001.

Tracy W. Olrich and Martha E. Ewing — "Life on Steroids: Bodybuilders Describe Their Perceptions of the Anabolic-Androgenic Steroid Use Period," *Sport Psychologist*, 1999.

Andrew Parkinson and Nick Evans — "Anabolic Androgenic Steroids: A Survey of 500 Users," *Medicine & Science in Sports & Exercise*, April 2006.

Paul Perry, Brian Lund, Michael Deninger, et al., — "Anabolic Steroid Use in Weightlifters and Bodybuilders: An Internet Survey of Drug Utilization," *Clinical Journal of Sport Medicine*, September 2005.

Paul J. Perry, Kathleen H. Andersen, and William R. Yates — "Illicit Anabolic Steroid Use in Athletes: A Case Series Analysis," *American Journal Sports Medicine*, July 1990.

Harrison Pope Jr., et al., — "Effects of Supraphysiologic Doses of Testosterone on Mood and Aggression in Normal Men," *Archives of General Psychiatry*, February 2000.

Harrison Pope Jr., et al.,	"Psychiatric and Medical Effects of Anabolic-Androgen Steroid Use," *Archives of General Psychiatry*, May 1994.
Jason Whitlock	"The War on Steroids Has No Juice," *ESPN*, February 2005.
Charles Yesalis, Michael Bahrke, James Wright	"Societal Alternatives to Anabolic Steroid Use," *Clinical Journal of Sport Medicine*, January 2000.

Index